P9-CJX-652

McCLANE'S NORTH AMERICAN FISH COOKERY

Also by A. J. McClane and Arie deZanger

The Encyclopedia of Fish Cookery

A. J. McClane

McCLANE'S NORTH AMERICAN FISH COOKERY

Photographs by Arie deZanger

Holt, Rinehart and Winston
New York

Published by Holt, Rinehart and Winston,
383 Madison Avenue, New York, New York 10017.

Published simultaneously in Canada by
Holt, Rinehart and Winston of Canada, Limited.

Library of Congress Cataloging in Publication Data

McClane, Albert Jules, 1922–
McClane's North American fish cookery.

1. Cookery (Sea food) 2. Cookery (Fish)
I. DeZanger, Arie. II. Title.
TX747.M214 641.6'92 80-23177

ISBN 0-03-043746-6

First Edition

Designer: Robert Reed
Printed in the United States of America
10 9 8 7 6 5 4 3 2 1

ACKNOWLEDGMENTS

Many people contributed their help in the compilation of this book. Arie deZanger and I "borrowed" various people's kitchens for days on end, and they really deserve a kind of award *merité*. Starting down east, I must thank Stanley Leen of Leen's Lodge, at Grand Lake Stream, Maine, who expedited our black-bass cookery experiments. Sailing upwind, I especially want to thank Executive Chef Michael Getty, Chef Scott Learnard, and owners Peter Rice and James Austin of the Dolphin Striker in Portsmouth, New Hampshire. For his delectable recipes my old friend Jerry Brody, owner of that Mecca of ichthyophiles, New York's Oyster Bar and Restaurant, and his erudite compatriot, George Morfogen. For always provocative conversations, John vonGlahn of the Fishery Council of New York. Also in Manhattan, for her original recipes and brilliant performance I must also thank Stephanie Stefanssen of the Sherry Institute of Spain. Up in the Catskill Mountains of New York at the Eldred Trout Preserve and Restaurant, my thanks goes to Manager Bill Ruppel, Vince Carberry, and our supportive kitchen expert, Home Economist Helen Feingold. In Annapolis, Maryland, where we worked in the test kitchen of the Office of Seafood Marketing, I want to thank Director Gordon Hallock and Seafood Specialist Margaret Cassell, Melanie Beckett, and Home Economist Marilyn Hellinger. In the Saint Petersburg kitchen of Florida's Department of Natural Resources my thanks to Home Economists Debra Sims, Vicky Murphy, and Pam Wallace. For provocative conversations in Florida, my thanks to master boat builder and fish *cuisinier* John Rybovitch. In San Francisco, at the Nob Hill Restaurant of the Mark Hopkins (one of my world favorites), special thanks goes to Executive Chef Antoine Huber and to General Manager Sandor Stangl, Food and Beverage Manager François Ane, and Mary McGeachy for their superlative assistance. My fishing pal, Larry Green, who teaches seafood cookery, contributed a unique recipe as well as his Pacific expertise.

Special thanks to technicians Wilma deZanger, our talented food stylist; to Winston Pheriot, studio assistant; and to Inez Krech for her superb editorial assistance.

We also wish to thank the following organizations for their assistance in preparing the photographs and recipes in this book.

Burdine's Department Store, Tampa, Florida
Champagne News and Information Bureau, New York, New York
Daniel's, Clearwater, Florida
Dolphin Striker Restaurant, Portsmouth, New Hampshire
Gump's, San Francisco, California
Hammacher Schlemmer, New York, New York
Inter-Continental Hotel Corporation, New York, New York
Irving Smith Kogan & Co., Inc., New York, New York
The Mark Hopkins Hotel, San Francisco, California
The Oyster Bar in Grand Central Station, New York, New York
The Poffertjes Pan, Sugar Loaf, New York

The Portfolio Catalogue, Sugar Loaf, New York
Rosser Reeves, Inc., New York, New York
Schieffelin Company, New York, New York
The Sherry Institute of Spain, New York, New York
Vera Linens, New York, New York
Williams-Sonoma, San Francisco, California
Woodward and Lothrop, Washington, D.C.

Although the author is wholly responsible for the recipes as described, their origins and or preparation for the photos are credited as follows:

Helen Feingold (Black Bass en Croûte, Black Bass Crêpes, Black Bass Fondue, Mexican Black Bass with Shrimp and Pepper Sauce, Mexican Black Bass with Salsa Cruda and Cheese, Black Bass Pudding with Sauterne Sauce, Muskokee Bass Stew, Tropical Black Bass en Gelée, Herb-Baked Black Bass, Black Bass Chaudfroid, Striped Bass Salad in Avocado Shells, Striped Bass Chowder, Striped Bass Fondue Bourguignonne, Crusty Striped Bass Steaks, Scandinavian-Style Perch with Shrimp Stuffing, Whitefish Mousse, Asparagus-Stuffed Trout Fillets with Mousseline Sauce, Baked Herb-Stuffed Trout, Green Fettucini with Trout Cream Sauce, Spaghetti with Trout Marinara, Souffléed Stuffed Trout, Walleye Baked with Ratatouille, and Japanese Prickly Shrimps); *Antoine Huber* (Petrale Sole en Papillote, Halibut Fillets in Lettuce Leaves, Mousse of Salmon and Petrale Sole, Baked Salmon with Asparagus, Scallops with Lemon Dressing, Coulibiac of Salmon, Sturgeon Fillet Mark Hopkins, Abalone with Grape Sauce, San Francisco Crab Soup, Pâté of Dungeness Crab with Sorrel, and Scallops and Mussels in Mustard Vinaigrette on Asparagus); *Stephanie Stefanssen* (Herbed Shad Roe en Papillote, Calamari Salad with Champagne Dressing, Cold Stuffed Mussels, Crayfish with Champagne, Lobster Salad with Poppy Seed Dressing, Bourride, Yosenabe, Shellfish in Patty Shells, Salmon Steaks with Sorrel Sauce, Stuffed Red Snapper Truffé, and Escabeche); *Inez Krech* (Cold Fish with Parsley Sauce, Spots en Papillote, Stir-Fried Croaker, Trout for Poor Young Anglers, Braised Swordfish with Tomatoes, Mussel Risotto, Scallops and Shrimps à la Chinoise, Crab and Leek Tarts, Bluefish Flamed with Vodka, Curried Fish Balls, Pickled Red Snapper, Red Snapper with Yogurt and Cucumber, and Salt Cod and Peanut Stew); *Oyster Bar* (Florida Grouper on Snow Peas with Hollandaise Sauce, Tournedos of Canadian Lotte with Noodles, Poached Ray with Brown Butter, Piccata of Mako Shark, and Sea Bass Grilled over Fennel Branches); *Vicky Murphy* and

Debra Sims (Triple Treat, Bluefish with Wild Rice and Mushroom Stuffing, Smoked Fish Logs, Mullet Turbans with Lemon-Rice Stuffing, Fried Mullet with Macadamia Nut Sauce, Crisp Broiled King Mackerel, Baked Pompano with Orange Butter Sauce, Rock Shrimp Newburg, Sweet and Sour Rock Shrimp Tails, Tilefish Fillets with Orange Sauce, French-Quarter Catfish with Béarnaise Sauce, and Bluefish with Mustard Butter); *Michael Getty* (Cod Pudding, Cod Florentine, Baked Haddock with Lobster Sauce, Fillet of Flounder Marguery, Flounder Appledore, Poached Wolffish with Shrimp-Curry Sauce, Clams Casino, Clam Fritters, Scallop Salad Dolphin Striker, Scallop and Shrimp Marucca, Shrimp and Mushroom Quiche, Hannah Mariner's Pie, and Baked Stuffed Lobster); *Jim Austin* (New England Fish Chowder); *Margaret Cassell, Marilyn Hellinger,* and *Melanie Beckett* (Old-Line Oyster Pie, Oysters Chancery, Hangtown Fry, Maryland Crab Cakes, Crêpes with Crab Sauce, Crabmeat Adventure, Crisfield Crab Fondue, and Crab Imperial); *Patrick Healy* (Patrick's Pompano); *Skippy Duncan Harwood* (Catch of the Day Stew); *Wilma deZanger* (Ukoy, Clam Poffertjes); *Larry Green* (Stuffed Rockfish Sesame); and *A. J. McClane* (Crabmeat Parfait, Red Drum Custard, Red Drum and Mushroom Pie, Catfish and Hushpuppies, Fisherman's Oyster Stew, and Walleye Quenelles with Cucumber Sauce).

CONTENTS

McCLANE'S NORTH AMERICAN FISH COOKERY

INTRODUCTION:

General Information about Fish

There are more than five hundred species of fish, crustaceans, and mollusks currently being marketed in the United States, and twice that number worldwide. The variety of our aquatic resources is enormous when compared with the relatively few terrestrial animals and fowl we utilize as food. This largesse has actually been counterproductive to the seafood industry in their attempts to develop markets for unfamiliar species. Unless one becomes a dedicated ichthyophile (which is not a bad idea), it is difficult, if not impossible, for the consumer to make the hundreds of qualitative judgments required in selecting from such a vast array. Until recently in the normal course of dining, the average household became familiar with perhaps only a dozen seafoods over a period of many years. But today America's oldest food industry is experiencing a veritable renaissance. Not only are restaurants across the nation reporting a steady increase in the sales of fishery products (from a low of 15 percent to as much as 40 percent since 1975), but previously ignored varieties of fish are also gaining widespread acceptance. In addition to what was once considered ethnic in our cuisine, such as the squid, sea urchin, or octopus, we now find tilefish, mullet, wolffish, shark, goosefish, rock shrimp, red crab, sand lance, macrobrachium, and many other delicacies at market and on menus. Although its high-protein, low-fat value is largely responsible for the growing popularity of fish, there is yet another reason for this heightened interest. More and more people are discovering what you and I already know, that "eating" is a gastronomic reward in itself; that is, they are seeking totally different dining experiences.

EDIBILITY FACTORS

Other than the five characteristics of a fresh fish—firm and elastic flesh, clear and full eyes, bright red gills, a clean odor, and unblemished skin—there are at least six edibility factors (compared with the more than forty organoleptic properties used in describing wines) that not only separate different species but in many cases also reveal similarities. In nearly all recipes a specific fish can have several substitutes. Obviously a yellow perch *en papillote* is not going to taste the same as a pompano *en papillote*, but they are sufficiently alike in having a mild, firm, and moderately flaky flesh to merit the same treatment.

The edibility factors that distinguish one species of fish from another are odor, flavor, texture, color, fat content, and moisture content. Odor and flavor are interrelated. When fresh out of the water, a fish has a mild, sweet odor. It may smell faintly like cucumber, celery, thyme, or even violets, and it is never offensive, except in the case of an Atlantic barracuda, which you are not foolish enough to eat in any case. On very rare occasions some marine fishes and, more particularly, shrimp may have a strong iodine aroma. Shrimp caught in totally saline water (30 parts per thousand) may feed on certain organisms that concentrate iodine. This occurs beyond the normal range of trawling operations—a random happening and no reflection on your fishmonger. Although somewhat unappetizing, it is nevertheless a fresh product. A truly bad shrimp would smell strongly of ammonia.

When cooked, all fresh fish have an appetizing aroma running the gamut from very mild to very intense, depending on the species and the method of preparation. Similarly, flavor varies from fragrantly mild, as in the yellowtail flounder, for example, to ocean strong, as in the bluefish. The more pronounced flavor of the latter is highly esteemed by true ichthyophiles. The most ancient civilizations used *garum* and other fermented fish liquids to exaggerate the flavor of bland seafoods and as a seasoning for animal meats, vegetables, and farinaceous products. Organoleptically, the range in fish flavor is comparable to that from a young Beaujolais to a robust Premier Grand Cru Burgundy—the one understated and the other clearly defined. There is no denying the papillary joy found in a delicate poached sole, but the more assertive taste of a Spanish mackerel roasted over a fruitwood fire until its skin sputters and crackles in a black and gold crust is quite another dining experience.

The fat content of a particular fish, which reduces to oil in cooking, contributes significantly to its flavor. We can say that a herring is usually a fatter fish than a rainbow trout, but this is not an absolute, since fat content varies within a species. Nor does high fat content reflect unfavorably on taste. Quite the contrary. Certain fish with a normally high fat content, such as herring, lake whitefish, pompano, salmon, lake trout, or Arctic char, are celebrated for their unique flavors. Both fat and water content are subject to seasonal variations related to the reproductive cycle (fat content decreases and water content increases during spawning). Consequently, there are prespawning and postspawning periods when a fish is "prime," with maximum fat and protein and minimum water and water solubles contained in the flesh.

Texture is a combination of flake size, density, and residual moisture after cooking. The meat of a fish is principally the lateral trunk muscle, which consists of angular, overlapping myotomes (muscle segments); the arrangement of their fibrils differs, as does the relation of other muscle components in various species. Large fishes, such as the king mackerel, wahoo, tunas, and swordfish, have prominent deep transverse tubular muscles close to their backbones. Visually, these appear as circular "tenderloins" within a fish steak—choice morsels that working fishermen sometimes excise for a personal feast in days of abundance. There is also a wedge of red subcutaneous muscle located just under the skin, identifiable as the "dark" meat. This has different contractile properties from the trunk muscle; while extremely nutritious, it can have an overly strong or bitter flavor in some species. The dark meat is usually a minor component in proportion to the other muscles and is barely evident in many fishes.

Except for the salmon and trout family, which generally has a range of flesh color in the red–orange spectrum, most fish have white meat. There are some other notable exceptions, such as the blood-red meat of bluefin and bigeye tuna (which looks like filet mignon when cooked on charcoal), the gray flesh of bluefish, and the often green flesh of that delectable Pacific sculpin, the cabezon (both turn white during cooking). In the case of salmon the consumer expects it to be "pink"; therefore a colorless fish such as a fall-run Chinook salmon or the often gray chum salmon is less desirable at market—and rightfully so. On the other hand, the pink-fleshed brown bullhead—a singular exception among catfishes—has less consumer appeal than its related species, as catfish are expected to be white. Some wild brook trout populations have yellow flesh that turns the color of an almond when cooked. Heat not only "fixes" the color but it separates the myomeres into characteristic shapes, thereby creating the texture—fine flake, medium flake, large flake, chunks, even crumbs, dry or moist, and firm or soft. If the fish is cooked with its skin intact, there will be no change in the texture, but there may be a distinct difference imparted to its flavor.

The skin of some fish—the eel, catfish, grouper, dolphin, triggerfish, goosefish, or tuna, for example—is so leathery that it's indigestible, although the meat in each case is a quality food. However, fish skin is edible in *most* species and, indeed, can be an exclamatory panache, as in a blue trout, or the traditional dividend, as in the crisp fried strips of salmon skin accompanying a correctly served gravlax. The skin of a fish is quite different from that of mammals. It is made up of living cells as far as the outermost layer, and a coating of slime makes it watertight. Along with the kidney it plays a role in the excretory function. Freshwater fish absorb water through their skin (saltwater fish drink it), so the flavor of their skin is an environmental product. When cooked, it can be delicious, but in rare instances it manifests a variety of unpleasant flavors. Nobody knows why, but the skin of a snook tastes like soap, yet the meat is so sweetly delicate that in years past it was sold to innocent Florida tourists as red snapper. (Because of the decline in our snook population and its more recent status as a protected game fish, this sinful practice has since been discontinued.)

A number of habitat conditions may affect the skin flavor of a local stock of fish, not necessarily some form of pollution (as we find in the petroleum wastes of the Hudson River) but dynamic factors in the ecosystem itself. The black bass, for example, a tremendously popular sport and food fish well represented in our recipe collection, often occurs in high-fertility lakes, where the algae plant is common. The skin of most black bass has a distinctly mossy or even muddy flavor; to a much lesser extent, so may the flesh. The chief offending agent is a colorless oil called geosmin, derived mainly from blue green algae. It is absorbed by the fish during periods when a lake or river is releasing nutrients that stimulate an algal bloom, usually in the spring or fall. Trout, carp, and catfish can be similarly affected, but the widely distributed largemouth bass is most often identified with this mossy flavor; yet when taken in clear water and shucked from its skin, the lean white meat is a delight at table. Being a game fish rather than a market product, it's simply a matter of selectivity on the part of the angler—who should know his source of supply.

HOW TO BUY FISH

Aside from freshness, another consideration when buying fish is the method by which it will be cooked according to your recipe requirements. The various ways a fish can be dressed do not produce the same qualitative results for a particular species. When a fish is steaked, for example, we have changed the axis of the muscle fibrils (relative to cooking) and thus the ultimate texture of the meat. When cut "across the grain," fish such as tuna, halibut, grouper, king mackerel, wahoo, swordfish, and salmon remain firm but tender and have less of a tendency to toughen under direct heat; in fillet form, however, these same species cook unevenly and become drier and more fibrous as the meat contracts. The contractile property of the myotomal muscle is considerable in a freshly caught fish, as many anglers discover at streamside when their whole trout, sputtering in butter, suddenly curls into a U shape and breaks apart in the frying pan. This is a normal and delicious reaction of the still-elastic fish protein.

Taxonomically, cross-cutting may be the only viable form of presentation, as is the case with our now-popular tilefish. Except for the heavy-boned rib cage (which is easily excised) and a double string of pin bones, the tilefish has an otherwise typical skeletal structure. (The pin bones are not as complex in arrangement as those in a pike or shad.) Tilefish can be filleted off the backbone in the usual fashion, but after skinning, you will find a series of unattached bones remaining in the midline from nape to tail in both fillets. These are simple to remove (with your finger you can feel the bone tips running in a straight line down the center of the fillet) by making two long wedge-shaped cuts on each side of the pin bones and lifting the strip out. This lengthwise cut halves each piece and results in four narrow but thick fillets from one fish. These are usually sliced crosswise on the bias into chunks on small tilefish (wonderful for chowder or stew) and into thinner, steaklike cuts from large tilefish of 20 pounds or more. The result is an unusual and delicate fish texture similar to crab meat. By being cut across the fibril axis, the tilefish is virtually tenderized.

The Japanese culinary art form of *sashimi* is based entirely upon properly cutting raw fish according to its density and musculature. Each species is sliced in stylized forms—*kaku giri*, or cubes; *hira giri*, or flat, thick slices; *usu zukuri*, or paper-thin slices; *ito zukuri*, or thread-shaped slices; and so on—to take advantage of the grain, which is tender in one direction and chewy in the other. While the importance of correct slicing is most apparent in raw fish (cut parallel to the muscle in a bluefin tuna and you will be chomping forever), the same principle applies when preparing cooked fish; hence, careful attention should be paid to selecting the proper form for an intended recipe.

At market, fish are sold in various forms, and any reliable retailer can provide some help in estimating individual portion sizes. I consider 8 ounces an average portion, unless you are serving an elaborate, multifaceted meal. Fish is "lighter" and more easily digested than animal meats; for a physically active adult 8 ounces is a satisfying serving as a main course. For hearty appetites even 12 ounces wouldn't qualify as a Roman banquet—if you've been on the water from dawn until dusk. Estimating portions is only confusing mathematically when buying a whole or drawn fish. Keep in mind that some types of fish have fragile bones, whereas others have heavy skeletons. Body cavity can be either large or small in proportion to muscle. Species such as red snapper, mutton snapper, blackfish (tautog), red grouper, and black grouper have very large heads, which may represent 25 percent of their total body weight. And although the head-length-to-body-length ratio is consistent within a species, different populations will be "meatier" at certain times of the year. The roe becomes very large near spawning time and may then comprise more than 20 percent of a fish's body weight. These variables must be compensated for; therefore, x number of pounds in a whole fish are not readily divided into y number of portions.

In the round, a 10-pound red or mutton snapper sounds grand enough to feed about eighteen people, but minus the skin, fins, viscera, and head, the actual yield in boneless meat is about 4½ pounds, or 45 percent—enough for merely eight people. By contrast, a prime 8-pound winter bluefish from North Carolina will yield exactly the same amount of meat—4½ pounds—since 54 percent of its total body weight is muscle. Fishmongers with skilled knives claim a 40 percent yield from tilefish and a 46 percent yield from groupers. However, to strike an average for all round-bodied fishes and amateur blades, a 40 percent yield is average. Despite their small heads and minimal bones, flatfishes generally produce less meat because of their thinner bodies. And the popular "gray sole" (witch flounder) yields only 33 or 34 percent in boneless meat. In other words, it requires 3 pounds of whole fish to obtain 1 pound of fillets —the reason for its prevailing high cost in the latter form. A prime Georges Bank "lemon sole" (winter flounder) will sometimes yield as much as 40 percent, as will a prime "fluke" (summer flounder). But again, to strike an average for flatfishes, consider 33 percent a viable figure. Obviously, any whole or drawn fish is no bargain compared with a fillet if the purchase price of the two forms is very similar. Heads, cheeks, skin, bones, throats, and even the cod's tongue can be utilized, but these products may not fit in with your menu. In any case, thinking in percentages is a reliable guide to buying.

The following market forms represent the most common methods of dressing fish:

Whole fish or "in the round." Purchased whole just as it comes from the water, this has to be scaled and gutted, with the fins and usually the head removed. The fish may then be turned into steaks or fillets or other types of cuts if required by the recipe. Personally, I prefer to leave the head and tail on for presentation unless I'm using the head in a stock. Certain miniature species—the sand lance, or "whitebait" (silversides), for example—are generally cooked whole without evisceration. One virtue in buying a whole fish is the dividends of head and bones for making stocks, and also the roe in some species, such as weakfish, mackerel, and cod. When buying a whole fish, estimate 16 ounces per serving, except for snappers, groupers, and tilefish, which can be compensated at about 20 ounces per serving. Flounders should be allowed 24 ounces. Sand lance and silversides can be figured in the average 8-ounce portion.

Drawn fish. This differs from a whole fish only in that the entrails are removed. A drawn fish must then be scaled and the fins, tail, and head removed (although tail and head may be left on for poached, baked, or broiled presentations). Of course, a drawn fish can subsequently be cut into any other form. While a whole fish is more of a dockside product, fresh out of the water, a drawn fish has better keeping qualities when delivered to your local market. For a drawn fish estimate 14 ounces per serving.

Dressed or pan-dressed fish. A dressed fish has been scaled and gutted by the fishmonger, with the head, tail, and fins removed (with head and tail left on, it is *whole-dressed*). It may also be skinned, as is usual for catfish, eel, or searobin. This is the most popular form for all small fish, since it's ready for cooking by any method. When buying, allow 8 ounces per serving.

Steaked fish. Cross-cut slices of a drawn or dressed fish, from ½ to 1½ inches thick, each steak includes a section of the backbone. This is a common market form for many of the larger species, such as tuna, halibut, white sea bass, mako, salmon, and swordfish. Steaks appear in three forms: *Rib steaks* are cross-cut pieces taken along the body cavity and therefore include some of the rib bones in the belly flaps. *Loin steaks* are cut from a point beyond the body cavity and are rounded in shape. In halibut and swordfish, which commonly weigh 60 to 300 pounds, the loin steaks are too large for a serving portion and are further cut into smaller pieces, so the meat may therefore show one or more straight edges and no bone. The third steak form is properly a cutlet: *Butterfly cutlets* are made from an unskinned fillet by first cutting crosswise through the meat almost to the skin, then making a second cut parallel to the first, slicing the skin. The two pieces remain attached by the joining skin. These alternate cuts are repeated along the fillet at equal ½- to 1½-inch intervals, depending on the thickness desired to obtain additional boneless steaks. This method is most suitable for thick fillets from round-bodied fishes, such as small tuna, king mackerel, wahoo, salmon, or large yellow pike (walleye). Allow 8 ounces per portion.

Fillet. This term refers to the sides of a fish cut lengthwise, parallel to, and free of the backbone. The rib cage can also be trimmed out with a thin, flexible blade by cutting downward under the bones and following their contour. Or the rib cage can be trimmed off by making a wide angular cut from the nape to the vent. Properly speaking, this is a *napecut fillet.* The skin may or may not be left on according to species and recipe requirements. If the fish is cut dorsally (along the back) without the knife penetrating the belly skin, so that the two fillets remain attached ventrally, it is known as a *butterfly fillet.* If the fish is cut ventrally and the two fillets are left attached on the dorsal side, it is a *block fillet* or *kited fillet.* The butterfly and block fillets are used mainly for smokehouse cookery, for planked fish when cooked on an open fire, and for stuffed fish dishes. In the case of flatfishes, these can be filleted into two pieces as *crosscut fillets,* or else each of these can be cut out in two pieces from a large fish, which are then called *quartercut fillets.* Quartercuts from the largest flatfish, the halibut, are known as *fletches.* Allow 8 ounces per portion.

Split fish. A whole fish cut lengthwise along the ventral side from throat to tail is called a split fish. The knife blade is pressed against and runs parallel to the backbone. The fish is gutted and scaled, with the head possibly removed. The backbone may or may not be left in (it supports the musculature in processing finnan haddie and salt cod). A split fish can also be deboned, thereby converting it into a block fillet by making a second cut parallel to the backbone on the side opposite before lifting it free. The rib cage is then excised by cutting laterally under the bones and following its contour. This requires some knowledge of gross fish anatomy with respect to individual species. Preparing trout for stuffing is easy with a split and deboned fish because of the trout's simple skeletal structure. Allow 8 ounces per portion.

Fish fingers. Strips of fresh fish cut from a skinless fillet into finger lengths by slicing across the grain, usually in ½-inch-wide pieces (they need not be uniform), this is primarily a home-customing method for preparing fish for deep frying. Commercially, in Europe, pieces are cut with a thickness equaling the width and are known as *tronçon* or *darne* in France, or *trancia* in Italy. This form is mainly used in pickling.

Fish sticks. Sticks differ from fingers in being mitered from a block of frozen fillets in uniform rectangular shapes. The sticks may be left uncooked or breaded and fried and sold frozen in cooked form. Each individual stick usually weighs about 1 ounce.

Dried fish. A fillet or split fish that has been sun-dried or air-dried, it is preserved by reducing the moisture content to prevent the growth of bacteria (water content below 25 percent) and to prevent mold (water content below 15 percent). This product is most often seen in ethnic markets of metropolitan cities. It should not be confused with the Japanese *namaboshi,* a moist short-term product (water content over 60 percent).

Dry-salted fish. This is a fillet, block fillet, or split fish that has been air-dried and salted for short- or long-term preservation. Although most popular in ethnic markets, it is the root product of the American fisheries industry. Salt cod seen as *bacalao* (Spanish), *bacalhau* (Portuguese), and *baccalà* (Italian) are the most popular forms, but mackerel, haddock, and other fishes can be dry-salted. It must be reconstituted with water before cooking, which increases its weight. Allow 6 ounces (precooked) per serving.

Frozen fish. To me, a fresh fish is one that I have personally caught and delivered to the kitchen the same day. During a lifetime of fishing this has been a normal sequence, except when we jig up a ritual Newfoundland cod on the tuna grounds and send it skidding to the galley for instant poaching. The succulent cod is splashed with melted butter flecked with Dijon mustard before the boat makes seaway again. Now *that* is fresh fish. The term *frozen fish* has become a kind of anathema, because so much depends on quality control versus the availability of a fresh product and the distance of its source of supply. I would prefer a properly treated frozen fish to a fish that has spent ten days in melty-ice transit between sea and table. However, any reputable market or restaurant, and especially a dedicated seafood house, will rely on stocks of fish that are locally indigenous and will present them to its patrons within forty-eight hours of dockside unloading.

I freeze some of my catch occasionally for the very good reason that certain species only make a brief or sporadic appearance along our coast. Some of these are fairly large, such as that giant mackerel the wahoo (known as *ono*, or "the sweet one," in Hawaii), which often weighs 40 to 80 pounds. Despite rare days of plenty in Florida, when the Gulf Stream seems alive with cavorting wahoo, they may otherwise be absent for months. Trimmed into butterfly cutlets, then ice-glazed and frozen, the tender white meat has been served as one of our most complimented party dishes. Not quite *à point* perhaps, but it never suffers in quality. Each summer I bring home a pair of Atlantic salmon from New Brunswick, which I steak and freeze at camp within minutes after being caught. Packed in dry ice, they arrive in perfect condition and provide many glorious meals long after the salmon season has passed. In addition, our freezer usually holds jolthead porgy, schoolmaster and lane snappers, cero mackerel and margate from the Bahamas, red-fleshed brook trout, and perhaps an Arctic char from Labrador—all exotic species that I simply cannot find on demand.

Although frozen products have a very definite role in the complete seafood kitchen, there are some species that I never freeze—striped bass, bluefish, spotted sea trout, and Atlantic mackerel among them. Nor would I send crab meat or lobster to the freezer. These will remain edible, but nucleotide changes bring about a rapid loss of texture and flavor—their essential attributes. They are also usually available in fresh form, so why bother?

Court bouillon and fish stock. While salted water is perfectly adequate for poaching, the ultimate flavor is achieved by using a court bouillon or short broth. This is made of aromatic vegetables, herbs, and spices simmered in water to which white wine has been added. There is no exact formula. The choice of ingredients is a matter of individual taste, as is the ratio of wine to water. The following is a basic court bouillon and should be made before you begin the poaching.

WHITE WINE COURT BOUILLON

8 cups water
4 cups dry white wine
2 onions, chopped
2 celery ribs with leaves, chopped
2 carrots, chunked
4 tablespoons chopped parsley stems
1 sprig fresh thyme, or ½ teaspoon dried thyme
2 bay leaves, broken up
1 garlic clove, whole
8 cracked peppercorns
1 tablespoon salt
12 thin lemon slices

Combine all ingredients in a large kettle and bring to a boil. Reduce heat and simmer for 40 minutes. Strain the broth through a sieve into your fish poacher.

With the back of a spoon, press down on the vegetables to extract all their juices into the broth. This makes about two quarts, which is a minimal amount. Double or triple the recipe according to the size of the fish, adding a little water, if necessary, to cover.

After poaching the fish, an innocent chef may pour the remaining broth down the sink. This is a total waste. Assuming that you came home with more than one fish and have other uses for the rest of the catch (or asked for some trimmings from your fishmonger), the broth can be converted into a rich fish stock or *fumet de poisson* that makes a wonderful base for sauces, aspics, soups, and chowders. All you need do is add some fish heads, bones, fins, and skins (make sure the skin has been scaled) to the leftover broth, and simmer over low heat for another half hour. Strain out all the trimmings after cooking. Fish stock is easy to make and keep on hand, frozen in pint- or quart-size plastic containers. As in a court bouillon there is no exact formula for making a fumet. I favor the ratio of 12 cups of broth to each 2 pounds of trimmings. To expedite the cooking of large heads they should be split lengthwise, and, regardless of size, the gills should always be removed. The trimmings in most fish markets are invariably from small fish, and these can be simmered for about 20 minutes to obtain their full essence. However, fishermen catching large groupers, snappers, striped bass, or any of the choice species with heavy bones may simmer the trimmings from 1 to 2 hours. A 10-pound head on a grouper is not unusual. To expedite cooking the heads of large fish, they should be split lengthwise from the underside. Regardless of size, the gills should always be removed.

Bottled clam juice is often used in place of fish stock or court bouillon. This is a convenient substitute, but it totally lacks the essence of a fumet and must be judiciously diluted with water, since the commercial product is quite salty. Clam juice is better than no stock, but the complete seafood kitchen should always have a few pints of fish stock or court bouillon in the freezer.

ABOUT THE RECIPES

There is a popular doctrine that a plain broiled fish or a poached fish sprinkled with lemon juice is the ultimate taste experience. I find it hard to disagree, although as a restaurant technique, broiling somehow defies the talents of many chefs, who fail to recognize when a fish is *al dente*. And despite the merit of such a pure concept, it would result in a monotonous cuisine when seafood is served with great frequency. There are also special occasions, a lunch or dinner party, for example, when a more fully developed dish is essential to the festivities. The silky counterpoint of sauces, the acidity of fruits in contrast to the alkalinity of a fresh fish, and the textures of nuts and vegetables are invaluable to an imaginative seafood chef. Indeed, the complements can inspire compliments.

Since the publication, in 1977, of *The Encyclopedia of Fish Cookery* I have made numerous fishing trips from Maine to California; this new collection of recipes represents a selection of regional specialties that I enjoyed along the way. In fact, when I review the contents, my taste buds blossom at the recollection of Crab Meat Adventure, Oysters Chancery, the Cod Pudding that I ate from an antique ceramic mold one evening, and the next morning in cold slices smeared with sweet pickle relish (a delectable form of aquatic junk food) while waiting to pull Jim Austin's lobster traps off windswept Kittery Point in Maine. You will also find an ethereal omelet version of Hangtown Fry that surpasses eggs scrambled with oysters. And there's a Smoked Fish Log that was intended as an hors d'oeuvre but transcends mere nibbling. Don't overlook Patrick's Pompano (he is Palm Beach's Patrick Healy, the talented young fish chef now with André Surmain) and the simple yet elegant Fried Mullet with Macadamia Nut Sauce.

One recipe that needs elaboration, because it relates to a unique style of dressing and trussing a fish, is Larry Green's Stuffed Rockfish Sesame (see page 49). The charcoal-cookery concept involved is one of the best I have tried for any large, round-bodied fish in whole form. Not only will it relieve the frustration of many weekend chefs who have tried to keep a big stuffed fish moist and intact on a hot grill, but this method even permits turning the fish without losing various parts to the firebox. Larry demonstrated the technique with Pacific rockfish and a striped bass of about 10 pounds. I have since tried it with equally large snappers and an Atlantic salmon of 22 pounds with great success. In practice the only limitation is the size of your charcoal unit.

The manual preparation is important and can be explained in six simple steps:

1. The whole fish must be drawn and scaled, but the head, tail, and all fins should be left intact. Make sure the body cavity is washed free of blood, then patted dry.

2. Run two long cuts down the entire length of the fish's back, one on each side of the dorsal fin, against the backbone. Do not cut through to the stomach cavity, but do cut from the back

almost to the anal (bottom) fin once the blade has passed the cavity. Leave the backbone inside the fish.

3. Season and stuff both the dorsal cuts and stomach cavity according to the recipe.

4. Lay a piece of aluminum foil on your counter that is the same length as the fish. Place strips of thick bacon vertically at 2-inch intervals over the entire length of the foil. Carefully place the fish on the foil over the strips. Match the now-covered bacon with parallel strips on top of the fish at the same interval. Twist or wrap the ends of bacon to form rings around the fish along the body. On a very large fish the bacon will not make a complete wrap (if so, see step 5).

5. Using butcher's string, truss the fish by securing each bacon ring, starting at the tail. Slip the string between the foil and bacon, then knot it off. Cinch it tightly, but keep the ingredients in place and maintain a fish shape. If the bacon strips were too small to wrap completely around the fish, slide extra slices under the string with a knife blade. The bacon fat prevents the string from burning and bastes the fish at the same time.

6. When the charcoal is red-hot, spread the briquets around the perimeter of the grill—hot coals should not be directly under the fish. Barbecue the fish on the foil with the cooker lid on and try to maintain a temperature of about 250° F. For a 10- to 12-pound fish allow 20 minutes for each side. Test with a fork in one of the dorsal cuts.

THE DONENESS FACTOR

Fish cooks faster than animal meats. In order to estimate cooking time, it has recently become fashionable to use what is known as the Canadian method: One merely measures the fish at its thickest point and allows 10 minutes of cooking time per inch at 450° F. Although this sometimes works, water content, oil content, and muscle density of individual species are all variables that significantly affect cooking time. To me, it merely codifies the disaster syndrome already prevalent in many kitchens. For many species 10 minutes to the inch is too long; I would find perfection within a shorter time span, but this is a subjective matter. Furthermore, when fish is cooked at the lower temperatures essential to compound dishes, the rule is no real help. It is far more reliable to learn how to "eyeball" a fish, then test it with a fork when it appears ready. Even the time-temperature suggestions in this book are only guidelines (which all recipes are in any case), based on what has been most successful for a particular chef. I still rely on the fork.

Admittedly, to "test with a fork for doneness" is a meaningless cliché unless you know what you are looking for. A fish that is already overcooked will "flake" as easily as one that is perfectly cooked—until it reaches an absolutely mummified stage. It is not the fact that it separates but what you *see* in the flake that is informative. A fish is ready for eating at the instant protein coagulates, when it turns from translucent to opaque.

Good results can be obtained if you modify the Canadian method by using the fork test. Test the fish with the fork at the 7-minute point and repeat at 1-minute intervals if necessary (remember to adjust the time according to thickness, 3½ minutes for ½-inch fish, 14 minutes for 2-inch fish, and so forth). Insert the tines in the thickest part of a fillet, parallel to and at the midline. Gently turn the fork and press inward. The still-juicy fish should show a trace of translucence, which will disappear before serving because the protein continues to coagulate after the fish is removed from the heat. If you are testing a fish steak, take your reading off-center. If you are baking or broiling a whole fish, insert the fork into the thickest part at the backbone; the easiest way to do this is to score the fish before cooking with several diagonal cuts spaced about 3 inches apart (do not score the thin tail section), cutting to, but not through, the backbone. Scoring not only assures more uniform heat penetration but allows an instant reference point for determining protein status.

Anybody who has learned to eyeball a hamburger can become just as expert at fork-testing fish.

BLACK BASS EN CROÛTE

one 2-pound black bass, dressed
salt and freshly ground pepper
dry white wine
2 tablespoons butter
4 shallots, minced
¼ pound fresh mushrooms, chopped
1 tablespoon lemon juice
¼ pound pâté with truffles
¼ teaspoon dried fines herbes
one 10-ounce package frozen patty shells, thawed overnight
1 egg, well beaten

Sprinkle bass with salt and pepper. Place in a skillet or fish poacher and add just enough wine to cover. Simmer, covered, for 15 minutes. Let bass cool in poaching liquid. Remove bass, drain, and remove skin, fins and their bones, and rib bones, but leave backbone, head, and tail in place. In a skillet, heat butter and sauté shallots for 5 minutes; add mushrooms and lemon juice and cook for another 5 minutes. Stir in pâté and herbs; set aside.

Stack three of the patty shells and, with a rolling pin, roll them out on a lightly floured surface to form a pastry sheet the same size as the bass. Place pastry on a baking sheet and place bass on pastry. Spread bass with a layer of the pâté mixture. Roll out remaining patty shells in the same manner and place the second sheet of pastry over the bass. Press pastry edges together and trim edges. Use trimmings to make ½-inch-wide strips. Brush bass with beaten egg and then arrange strips on top. Brush with egg again. Bake in a preheated 400°F. oven for 30 to 35 minutes, or until pastry is puffed and browned.

Serve with cherry tomatoes sautéed in butter and chopped chives, and steamed broccoli and cauliflower flowerets.

MAKES 2 SERVINGS.

Scales present
Connected
No teeth on tongue
Jaw to mid-point of pupil
20-21 scale rows below lateral line
Scales present
Northern Smallmouth Bass
Connected
Opercular spot

BLACK BASS CRÊPES

Crêpes

4 eggs
½ teaspoon curry powder
½ teaspoon salt
1 cup milk
1 cup unsifted flour

Filling

2 pounds black bass fillets, skinned
salt and freshly ground white pepper
1 cup dry white wine
approximately 3 cups half-and-half
¼ pound (1 stick) butter
½ cup flour
½ pound chopped fresh broccoli, cooked

⅓ cup grated Parmesan cheese

In a bowl, combine all crêpe ingredients and beat until smooth. Let stand for 1 hour. Heat a 7-inch skillet or crêpe pan and butter lightly. Stir batter thoroughly; spoon about 2 tablespoonfuls into the skillet and rotate pan to spread a thin layer of batter over the entire bottom of the pan. Brown crêpe on one side, then turn out onto a piece of aluminum foil. Butter pan again and continue making crêpes. There should be 18 crêpes.

Sprinkle bass fillets with salt and pepper. Place in a large skillet and add wine. Gently simmer, covered, for 20 to 25 minutes. Let bass cool in liquid. Remove fish and reserve poaching liquid. Break fillets into bite-size pieces. Add enough half-and-half to poaching liquid to make 4 cups. In a saucepan, melt butter and stir in flour. Add poaching liquid and half-and-half mixture and cook, stirring, over low heat until sauce thickens and bubbles. Add salt and pepper to taste. Place half of this sauce in a bowl and add the bass pieces and broccoli; use this mixture to fill the crêpes.

Spoon about 3 tablespoons filling into each crêpe and roll up. Place filled crêpes side by side, seam side down, in a lightly greased shallow oblong casserole. Spoon remaining sauce over the crêpes and sprinkle with cheese. Bake in a preheated 350°F. oven for 35 minutes, or until lightly browned. Garnish with capers.

MAKES 6 SERVINGS.

OF THE

BLACK BASS FONDUE

2 to 3 pounds black bass fillets, skinned
3 eggs, separated
1 cup beer
1 cup unsifted flour
1 teaspoon salt
1 teaspoon paprika
dash of garlic powder
peanut oil for deep frying
Hot Sauce (recipe follows)
Tartar Sauce (recipe follows)
Curry Sauce (recipe follows)

In a bowl, mix egg yolks, beer, flour, salt, paprika, and garlic powder. When ready to serve, in another bowl, beat egg whites until stiff and fold whites into beer mixture. Cut fillets into bite-size pieces. Spear with fondue forks and dip into batter. In a tabletop fondue pot, heat oil to 360°F., drop in fish pieces, and deep fry for 5 or 6 minutes, or until pieces are golden brown and crisp. Each guest can cook his or her own at the table. Serve with one or several of the sauces.

MAKES 4 TO 6 SERVINGS.

Hot Sauce

Mix ½ cup chili sauce with 2 tablespoons thawed frozen concentrated orange juice and 1 tablespoon prepared white horseradish.

MAKES ½ CUP.

Tartar Sauce

Mix ¾ cup mayonnaise with 1 tablespoon lemon juice, 1 tablespoon drained capers, and ¼ cup well-drained pickle relish.

MAKES 1 CUP.

Curry Sauce

Mix ⅓ cup mayonnaise with ⅓ cup sour cream, 1 teaspoon curry powder, and ⅓ cup shredded peeled green apple. Add salt to taste.

MAKES 1 CUP.

MEXICAN BLACK BASS WITH SHRIMP AND PEPPER SAUCE

two 2-pound black bass, dressed
salt and freshly ground pepper
¼ cup olive oil
2 cloves garlic, chopped
1 red bell pepper, cut into ½-inch-wide strips
1 green bell pepper, cut into ½-inch-wide strips
1 red onion, coarsely chopped
1 pound fresh shrimps, shelled and deveined
4 ounces canned sweet green chilies, drained and chopped
½ cup quartered, pitted black olives
1½ cups tomato juice
2 tablespoons flour

Place bass in a greased shallow baking pan. Sprinkle with salt and pepper. Bake in a preheated 350°F. oven for 20 to 25 minutes. Remove from oven and let cool. Strip off skin and return fish to baking pan; set aside. In a large skillet, heat oil and sauté garlic, red and green peppers, and onion for 5 minutes. Add shrimps, chilies, and olives. In a bowl, mix tomato juice and flour until smooth, then stir into skillet. Simmer, stirring, until sauce thickens slightly. Spoon sauce over bass and replace in oven. Bake for another 15 to 20 minutes, or until bass is cooked.

MAKES 4 SERVINGS.

MEXICAN BLACK BASS WITH SALSA CRUDA AND CHEESE

two 2- to 2½-pound black bass
  whole-dressed, fins intact
¼ cup olive oil
2 cloves garlic, chopped
1 small onion, chopped
4 large ripe tomatoes, chopped
4 ounces canned sweet green chilies,
  drained and finely chopped
salt and freshly ground pepper to taste
¾ pound Monterey Jack cheese,
  grated (3 cups)
garnish: roasted red peppers, ¼ cup melted
  butter, fresh parsley, red onion

In a saucepan, heat oil, and sauté garlic and onion for 5 minutes. Add tomatoes and chilies, and simmer, stirring occasionally, for 20 minutes. Meanwhile, oil bottom of a shallow baking pan and both sides of bass. Bake bass in preheated 350°F. oven for 15 minutes, or until skin loosens. Remove from oven and strip off skin. Pluck out fins except tail, removing basal bones. Season the sauce with salt and pepper and spoon it over the bass. Sprinkle with cheese, and bake for another 20 minutes. Transfer to a serving platter and garnish with roasted red peppers sautéed in melted butter, parsley sprigs, and red onion rings.

MAKES 4 SERVINGS.

BLACK BASS PUDDING WITH SAUTERNE SAUCE

one 2- to 2½-pound black bass, gutted
and scaled, fins intact
salt
approximately 1½ cups Sauterne
¼ cup butter
2 tablespoons chopped green pepper
2 tablespoons chopped pimiento
2 tablespoons chopped celery leaves
2 tablespoons chopped fresh chives
4 cups plain croutons
3 eggs, well beaten
1 teaspoon Worcestershire sauce
2 cups half-and-half
fine dry bread crumbs

Sprinkle bass with salt inside and out. Place fish in a large, deep skillet or poacher and add enough Sauterne to half cover fish. Simmer, covered, for 20 to 25 minutes. Let bass cool in poaching liquid. Remove fish, and reserve 1 cup poaching liquid for sauce. Skin bass and pluck out fins, removing basal bones. Break meat into small pieces. In a saucepan, melt butter and sauté green pepper, pimiento, celery leaves, and chives for 5 minutes. Scrape mixture into a bowl and stir in bass pieces and croutons. In a separate bowl, beat eggs with Worcestershire sauce, 1 teaspoon salt, and half-and-half. Stir this mixture into fish. Let stand for 15 minutes. Meanwhile make Sauterne Sauce (recipe follows) and keep warm.

Butter two 3-cup fish molds generously, and sprinkle inside of molds with dry bread crumbs. Shake out excess crumbs. Fill molds with bass mixture. Bake in a preheated 350°F. oven for 40 to 45 minutes. Loosen edges of the pudding with the tip of a knife and unmold onto a serving platter. Top with Sauterne Sauce.

MAKES 6 SERVINGS.

Sauterne Sauce

In a saucepan, melt ¼ cup butter and stir in ¼ cup flour. Gradually stir in 1 cup reserved poaching liquid and 1½ cups heavy cream. Continue stirring over medium heat until sauce thickens and bubbles. Season with salt and pepper.

MAKES ABOUT 2½ CUPS.

MUSKOKEE BASS STEW

1½ to 2 pounds black bass fillets, skinned
⅓ cup corn oil
3 onions, finely chopped
3 cloves garlic, chopped
4 slices bacon, diced
1 green pepper, chopped
½ pound fresh mushrooms, sliced
1½ cups chopped celery with leaves
4 large ripe tomatoes, diced
½ teaspoon dried oregano, or 6 branches fresh oregano
½ teaspoon dried sage, or 3 clusters fresh sage leaves
1 bay leaf
1¾ cups chicken broth
1 cup dry white wine
1 cup tomato puree
salt and freshly ground black pepper to taste

In a large saucepan, heat oil and sauté onions, garlic, bacon, green pepper, mushrooms, and celery for 5 to 10 minutes, or until lightly browned. Add tomatoes, oregano, sage, bay leaf, chicken broth, wine, and tomato puree. Simmer, covered, for 15 to 20 minutes, until vegetables are tender. Cut bass fillets into bite-size pieces and add to stew. Simmer, covered, for another 15 minutes. Remove herbs (if fresh are used) and bay leaf. Season with salt and pepper. Serve in large bowls with slices of crusty bread.

MAKES 6 SERVINGS.

TROPICAL BLACK BASS EN GELÉE

two 2-pound black bass, dressed
chicken broth
juice of 1 lime
salt to taste
2 navel oranges, peeled and sectioned
stuffed green olive slices
quartered black olives
2 envelopes unflavored gelatin
garnish: lime, papaya, fern sprigs

Place bass in a skillet or poacher. Add just enough chicken broth to cover bass, and add lime juice and salt. Gently simmer, covered, for 25 to 30 minutes, or until bass is cooked. Let cool in poaching liquid. Remove bass, and strain and reserve 3 cups poaching liquid. Strip off skin, and remove any small bones, but leave backbone, tail, and head intact. Place bass on a rack set over a shallow pan and chill. Place bass on serving platter and decorate them with orange sections and olives; chill.

In a saucepan, stir gelatin into 1 cup reserved poaching liquid. Stir over low heat until gelatin is dissolved. Stir in remaining 2 cups poaching liquid. Let cool, then chill until gelatin becomes syrupy. Spoon a thin layer of gelatin over bass; chill until layer is firm. Spoon on another layer and chill. Repeat until bass are completely covered with aspic. Chill until ready to serve.

Serve garnished with lime wedges and surrounded by ripe papaya slices that have been sprinkled with lime juice. Decorate with sprigs of fern.

MAKES 4 SERVINGS.

HERB-BAKED BLACK BASS

two 2- to 3-pound black bass, gutted
and scaled, fins intact
salt and freshly ground pepper
⅓ cup butter, melted
rind of 1 lemon, grated
1 tablespoon minced fresh tarragon,
or 1 teaspoon dried tarragon
1 tablespoon minced fresh oregano,
or 1 teaspoon dried oregano
1 tablespoon minced fresh sage, or
1 teaspoon dried sage
1 tablespoon minced fresh parsley,
or 1 teaspoon dried parsley

Oil bottom of a shallow baking pan and both sides of bass. Cook bass in preheated 350°F. oven for 15 minutes, or until skin loosens. Remove from oven and strip off skin. Pluck out fins except the tail, removing basal bones. Mix butter with lemon rind and herbs. Brush over bass in baking pan. Bake for another 20 to 25 minutes. While bass are baking, make Orange Sauce and keep warm.

When bass are ready, arrange on serving platter and spoon on sauce. Garnish with sprigs of fresh oregano, tarragon, sage, and parsley.

MAKES 4 SERVINGS.

Orange Sauce

2 tablespoons butter
1 small onion, grated
¼ cup flour
2 cups orange juice
¼ cup orange liqueur
rind of 1 orange, slivered
1 teaspoon dry mustard
salt and freshly ground pepper

In a saucepan, melt butter, add onion, and sauté for 2 to 3 minutes. Stir in flour. Gradually stir in orange juice and liqueur. Add orange rind and dry mustard. Stir over medium heat until sauce thickens and bubbles. Season with salt and pepper to taste.

MAKES ABOUT 2 CUPS.

BLACK BASS CHAUDFROID

two 2- to 3-pound black bass, gutted
and scaled, fins intact
salt
freshly ground pepper
1 cup champagne
chicken broth
bouquet garni (sprigs of fresh thyme,
parsley, and tarragon;
bay leaf)
1 envelope unflavored gelatin
1 cup mayonnaise
garnish: lettuce, black olives, pimiento,
green pepper, fresh tarragon,
lemon

Sprinkle bass with salt inside and out. Place fish in a very large, deep skillet or poacher. Add champagne and just enough chicken broth to cover bass. Add the bouquet garni. Gently simmer, covered, for 25 to 30 minutes. Let cool in poaching liquid. Remove bass, and strain and reserve 1 cup poaching liquid. Strip off skin, and remove all fins except the tail, eliminating the basal bones. Place bass on a rack set over a shallow pan and chill.

In a saucepan, mix gelatin and reserved poaching liquid. Stir over low heat until gelatin is dissolved. Beat in mayonnaise. Chill mixture until it thickens slightly and mounds when dropped from a spoon. Spoon gelatin over bass, coating them completely. Chill until layer is firm, then coat again until gelatin is smooth and even. Refrigerate until serving time.

Arrange bass on a bed of lettuce leaves and garnish with sliced black olives, strips of pimiento and green pepper, and fresh tarragon sprigs. Surround with seasoned cooked and chilled vegetables, such as asparagus tips, peas, and whole baby carrots. Add lemon slices.

MAKES 4 TO 6 SERVINGS.

STRIPED BASS SALAD IN AVOCADO SHELLS

3 pounds striped bass fillets, skinned
1 teaspoon salt
4 whole cloves
4 peppercorns
4 allspice berries
1 bay leaf
1 lemon, sliced
1 cup dry white wine
½ cup minced celery
1 carrot, shredded
6 radishes, sliced
1 ripe tomato, cored and diced
½ cup oil
¼ cup lemon juice
salt and freshly ground pepper to taste
3 ripe avocados, halved
garnish: lettuce, cherry tomatoes,
lime slices

Sprinkle bass with salt. Wrap fillets in cheesecloth and loosely tie ends together. Place in a very large, deep skillet and add spices wrapped in separate piece of cheesecloth, bay leaf, and lemon. Add wine and just enough water to cover. Bring to a boil, then gently simmer, covered, for 30 minutes. Let bass cool in poaching liquid; drain. Flake fish into a bowl. Add celery, carrot, radishes, tomato, oil, and lemon juice. Toss gently and season with salt and pepper. Chill.

Spoon fish mixture into avocado halves. Place filled halves on lettuce leaves. Garnish with cherry tomatoes and lime slices.

MAKES 6 SERVINGS.

STRIPED BASS CHOWDER

one 3-pound striped bass,
whole-dressed
3 cups water
salt
1 teaspoon dried thyme
1 onion, sliced
1 carrot, sliced
2 potatoes, peeled and diced
2 cups milk
2 cups half-and-half
¼ cup butter or margarine,
softened
¼ cup flour
freshly ground pepper to taste
garnish: butter, chives

Remove bass fillets for chowder. Place head, skin, and bones in a large saucepan. Add water, 1 teaspoon salt, thyme, onion, and carrot. Bring to a boil, then reduce heat, and gently simmer, covered, for 20 minutes. Strain broth and return to saucepan. Remove vegetables from strainer and add to broth. Add potatoes, cover, and simmer for 15 minutes, or until potatoes are tender. Stir in milk and half-and-half. In a bowl, mix butter or margarine and flour into a paste. Add to chowder, stirring until paste is melted and chowder thickens slightly. Cut reserved fillets into 1-inch cubes and add to chowder. Simmer for 5 minutes. Season with salt and pepper.

Top each serving with a pat of butter and some chives. Serve with chowder crackers.

MAKES 6 SERVINGS.

STRIPED BASS FONDUE BOURGUIGNONNE

3 pounds striped bass fillets
Curry Sauce (recipe follows)
salt and freshly ground pepper
2 eggs
1 cup milk
¾ cup flour
oil or fat for deep frying

Prepare Curry Sauce ahead of time. Cut bass fillets into 1-inch chunks. Sprinkle with salt and pepper. In a bowl, beat eggs with ½ teaspoon salt until smooth. Beat in milk and then beat in flour. (The batter should have the consistency of thick cream.) Heat oil or fat in a fondue pot to 360° to 380°F. Spear bass cubes on fondue forks and dip into batter. Plunge cubes into hot oil or fat and cook for 4 to 5 minutes, or until richly browned. Dip bass into sauce and eat while fish is hot.

MAKES 6 SERVINGS.

Curry Sauce

1 cup sour cream
1 cup mayonnaise
2 teaspoons curry powder
⅓ cup pickle relish, well drained

Combine all ingredients and stir until well blended. Chill in refrigerator.

MAKES ABOUT 2 CUPS.

CROCK

CRUSTY STRIPED BASS STEAKS

six 1-inch-thick striped bass steaks
Sauterne Sauce (recipe follows)
salt and freshly ground pepper
1 egg, well beaten
1½ cups cornflake crumbs
¼ cup butter or margarine
⅓ cup oil
garnish: fresh parsley, cherry tomatoes

Make Sauterne Sauce and keep warm. Sprinkle steaks with salt and pepper. Dip steaks into egg, then into cornflake crumbs, pressing crumbs firmly to make them adhere. In a large, heavy skillet, heat butter or margarine and oil. Fry steaks slowly until richly browned on both sides. Drain on absorbent paper. Place steaks on serving platter. Spoon sauce over fish. Garnish with parsley sprigs and cherry tomatoes.

MAKES 6 SERVINGS.

Sauterne Sauce

2 cups milk
1 teaspoon salt
¼ teaspoon freshly ground white pepper
¼ teaspoon dry mustard
¼ cup butter or margarine, softened
¼ cup flour
¼ cup Sauterne
2 eggs, hard-cooked and chopped

In a saucepan, heat milk, salt, pepper, and mustard. Knead butter or margarine and flour to form a smooth paste. Drop paste lump into hot liquid. Cook, stirring, over low heat until lump melts and sauce thickens. Stir in Sauterne and chopped eggs. Season sauce with additional salt and pepper to taste if needed.

MAKES ABOUT 2½ CUPS.

SEA BASS GRILLED OVER FENNEL BRANCHES

one 2- to 3-pound drawn black sea bass
salt and freshly ground pepper
dried fennel branches
2 tablespoons oil
anisette

Rinse fish and dry thoroughly. Season inside and out with salt and pepper and stuff with a fennel branch. Prepare a charcoal broiler with a base layer of fennel branches and ignite them. Keep adding more fennel. When burning well, place fish on a wire rack, brush fish with oil, and place the rack on the broiler. Broil fish for 6 minutes on one side and 8 minutes on the other side. To serve, put additional branches of fennel on a fireproof serving platter. Warm the platter and put fish on top. Sprinkle fish with anisette, ignite the liqueur, and serve the sea bass flaming.

MAKES 4 SERVINGS.

NOTE: *The Atlantic black sea bass is the sole member of the Pacific rockfish family to be found in Atlantic waters. Any of the rockfishes may be utilized in this recipe.*

STUFFED ROCKFISH SESAME

one 6-pound rockfish, dressed
1/4 cup lemon juice
1/4 cup soy sauce
freshly ground black pepper
garlic salt
2 tablespoons minced fresh basil
3 onions, cut into 1/4-inch-thick slices
3 green apples, cut into 1/4-inch-thick slices
3 oranges, cut into 1/4-inch-thick slices
3 lemons, cut into 1/4-inch-thick slices
1 bunch fresh parsley sprigs
1/2 cup sesame seed oil
1/2 cup raw sesame seeds
1/2 pound bacon (10 pieces), thickly sliced
1/4 cup paprika
oil for deep frying (optional)
2 Maraschino cherries
garnish: watercress and fresh strawberries

Dress fish according to directions on page 15–16. Mix lemon juice and soy sauce and brush generously over the cuts on the fish and in the body cavity. Sprinkle same areas with black pepper, garlic salt, and basil. Stuff cavity with enough onion, apple, orange, and lemon slices and parsley sprigs to restore the full-bodied shape of the fish. Brush some of the sesame oil in the exposed areas of the cuts on the fish, and sprinkle generously with sesame seeds, reserving some. Arrange slices of onion, apple, orange, and lemon along each cut. Use bacon slices to truss the fish according to directions on page 15–16. Sprinkle entire fish with remaining sesame seeds, and sprinkle paprika between bacon strips.

Barbecue the fish on a charcoal grill (preferable method) at 250° to 275°F. with the hood down. Cook for 30 minutes, turning the fish at the halfway point, or bake in a preheated oven, at the same temperature, for the same period of time. Test for doneness. When finished, arrange fish on a large silver platter. Cut strings and remove. Replace eyes of fish with Maraschino cherries. Garnish platter with watercress sprigs and large strawberries.

MAKES 6 SERVINGS.

FLORIDA GROUPER ON SNOW PEAS WITH HOLLANDAISE SAUCE

four 10-ounce pieces boned fresh grouper
fine bread crumbs
oil
8 ounces fresh snow peas
1 shallot, minced
¼ pound (1 stick) butter
1 cup Hollandaise Sauce, heated

Coat grouper lightly with bread crumbs and brush with oil. Place fish on a rack and broil for about 15 minutes, or until done to your taste. Meanwhile, blanch snow peas in boiling salted water for 1 minute; drain. In a skillet, heat half the butter and sauté the shallot until soft. Add blanched snow peas and remaining butter, and season with salt. Arrange snow peas on a serving plate, place grouper on the bed of snow peas, and top with hollandaise sauce.

MAKES 4 SERVINGS.

Hollandaise Sauce

2 egg yolks
dash of salt
dash of cayenne pepper
juice of ½ lemon
2 tablespoons hot water
¼ pound butter

Rinse a blender container with very hot water and dry it. Drop egg yolks, seasonings, lemon juice, and hot water into the container. Melt butter in a saucepan over low heat until it is almost bubbling. Cover blender container and whirl egg yolks and seasonings at medium speed until foamy. Remove the center cap from the cover. With the machine running at high speed, slowly pour in the melted butter. When the butter is all added, the sauce is ready. Do not blend further. Spoon the sauce into a bowl, and set the bowl in a *bain marie* filled with very hot, not simmering, water. The *bain marie* should be set in a warm place, but not over heat. Do not reheat the sauce; it should be served warm, not hot.

MAKES ABOUT 1 CUP.

BLUEFISH WITH WILD RICE AND MUSHROOM STUFFING

3 pounds dressed bluefish
1½ teaspoons salt
Wild Rice and Mushroom Stuffing
(recipe follows)
2 tablespoons oil

Make Wild Rice and Mushroom Stuffing. Wash and dry fish. Sprinkle inside and out with salt. Stuff fish loosely. Close openings with small skewers or food picks. Place fish on a well-greased baking pan and brush with oil. Bake in a preheated 350°F. oven for 30 to 35 minutes, or until fish flakes easily when tested with a fork. Baste occasionally with oil. Remove skewers.

MAKES 6 SERVINGS.

Wild Rice and Mushroom Stuffing

4 ounces uncooked wild rice
¼ cup margarine or oil
½ cup chopped onion
½ cup chopped celery
½ cup sliced mushrooms
¼ cup chopped fresh parsley
¼ teaspoon freshly ground pepper

Cook wild rice according to directions on package; set aside. In a heavy skillet, heat margarine or oil and sauté vegetables until tender. Combine all ingredients and mix thoroughly.

MAKES ABOUT 2½ CUPS.

BLUEFISH FLAMED WITH VODKA

one 3-pound bluefish, whole-dressed
salt and freshly ground white pepper
¼ cup olive oil
6 large shallots, minced
½ pound fresh mushrooms, sliced
6 large oysters, drained
2 pimientos, rinsed and chopped
1½ to 2 cups small white bread cubes
juice and grated rind of 1 lemon
¼ to ½ cup dry white wine
20 bay leaves
⅓ cup vodka

Wipe bluefish with damp paper towel and sprinkle inside with salt and pepper. Use 1 tablespoon of the oil to coat a baking dish large enough to hold the fish. In a saucepan, heat 2 tablespoons of the oil and sauté shallots and mushrooms until shallots are translucent. Cut each oyster into three or four pieces and add to shallots and mushrooms. Add pimientos. Sauté for 1 minute, then gently stir in bread cubes and remove from heat. Season dressing with salt and pepper and stuff the fish. Close the opening with small skewers and lace closed with white string or linen thread. Place fish in baking dish. Mix lemon juice and remaining tablespoon of oil and use to brush outside of fins. Sprinkle grated lemon rind over all. Pour wine around fish (the amount needed depends on the size and shape of the dish; there should be just enough to moisten the bottom of the fish). Cover dish with foil and bake in a preheated 350°F. oven for 35 minutes, or until fish tests done.

Remove dish from oven; unless dish is metal, cover the edges with crimped foil. Arrange bay leaves around bluefish and pour vodka over. Place baking dish in a preheated broiler about 5 inches from source of heat and broil until vodka is ignited and bay leaves are charred on the edges. As soon as flames die out, serve in the baking dish or carefully transfer to a large platter.

MAKES 6 TO 8 SERVINGS.

BLUEFISH WITH MUSTARD BUTTER

2 pounds bluefish fillets or other fish fillets, skinned
3 cups water
¾ cup plus 3 tablespoons lemon juice
6 tablespoons butter or margarine, melted
4 teaspoons Dijon mustard
¾ teaspoon salt
½ teaspoon paprika
garnish: fresh parsley

Cut fillets into serving-size portions. Place fillets in a single layer in a baking dish. Combine water and ¾ cup lemon juice; pour over fish. Marinate in refrigerator for 20 minutes.

Combine butter or margarine, 3 tablespoons lemon juice, mustard, salt, and paprika; mix well. Place fish on a well-greased broiler pan, and brush generously with mustard mixture, reserving some for later. Broil 4 inches from source of heat for 4 to 6 minutes, then turn carefully. Brush generously with sauce and broil for 4 to 6 minutes longer, or until fish flakes easily when tested with a fork. Sprinkle fish with fresh parsley. Warm remaining sauce and serve with fish.

MAKES 6 SERVINGS.

CURRIED FISH BALLS

4 pounds dressed striped bass, Pacific
rockfish, or red snapper,
including head and bones
2 teaspoons salt
1 cup dry white wine
1 bay leaf
½ cup peanut oil
½ pound onions, minced
2 teaspoons curry powder
2 tablespoons minced fresh parsley
1 teaspoon minced fresh mint
½ teaspoon minced fresh savory, or
¼ teaspoon dried savory
2 eggs, beaten just to mix
½ to 1 cup fresh white bread crumbs
2 cups tomato juice
juice of 1 lemon

Put fish in a poacher, or cut into chunks and put in a deep kettle. Add salt, wine, bay leaf, and enough water to cover the fish. Bring to a boil, reduce to a simmer, and cook fish until just done. Transfer fish to a large platter; reserve cooking liquid. When fish is cool enough to handle, remove skin and bones and return these to poacher or kettle; set remaining meat aside. Again bring to a boil, and simmer until stock is reduced to two-thirds. Pour through a fine sieve lined with a dampened cloth; set aside. Flake fish into a bowl.

In a skillet, heat half the oil and sauté onions until translucent. Add curry powder and cook, stirring, until browned; mix into fish. Add minced herbs, beaten eggs, and ½ cup bread crumbs. (If necessary, add more bread crumbs to make a mixture firm enough to mold.) Shape into balls the size of limes. In skillet, heat remaining oil and sauté fish balls until golden brown on all sides. In a bowl, combine 2 cups of the fish stock, the tomato juice, and the lemon juice, and carefully pour around the fish balls. Cover skillet and simmer for 1 hour, or until sauce is reduced to half. Occasionally turn fish balls around in the sauce to cook evenly. If necessary, add more of the fish stock, ½ cup at a time. Serve in a nest of spinach noodles, with some sauce poured over.

MAKES 4 TO 6 SERVINGS.

STUFFED RED SNAPPER TRUFFÉ

one 6- to 8-pound red snapper, dressed
and boned, head and tail intact
salt and freshly ground pepper
2 fillets of whiting
1 egg white
2 tablespoons minced truffles
¾ cup champagne
¼ cup butter or margarine, melted
juice of 1 lemon
Hollandaise Sauce (p. 51)
garnish: baked patty shells, fresh
asparagus tips, Beluga caviar,
hard-cooked egg yolk, lemon,
fresh mushroom caps

Sprinkle red snapper inside and out with salt and pepper. In a food processor, blend whiting fillets until they achieve a pastelike consistency. Add egg white and truffles and mix well. Add ½ teaspoon salt. Use mixture to stuff red snapper. Sew or skewer openings. Place snapper on a greased foil-lined shallow baking pan.

In a bowl, combine champagne, butter or margarine, and lemon juice, and pour over red snapper. Bake in a preheated 350°F. oven for 40 to 50 minutes, spooning pan juices over fish frequently. Transfer fish to a large platter. Serve with hollandaise sauce on the side. Garnish with patty shells filled with asparagus tips and Beluga caviar, sprinkled with sieved egg yolk. Add lemon slices topped with fluted mushrooms.

MAKES 6 SERVINGS.

PICKLED RED SNAPPER

2 pounds boned red snapper fillets
1 cup flour
2 teaspoons salt
¼ teaspoon freshly ground pepper
½ cup olive oil
¾ pound onions, chopped
¾ pound green peppers, chopped
½ cup fresh parsley sprigs
10 peppercorns
10 coriander berries
1 teaspoon cuminseed
1 teaspoon whole saffron
1 cup dry white wine
juice and grated rind of 3 lemons
1 cup pitted black olives
6 bay leaves
garnish: lettuce

Cut fillets into crosswise pieces about 1 inch wide. In a paper or plastic bag, mix flour, salt, and pepper; add fish pieces, a few at a time, and shake in the flour mixture. Pieces should be only lightly coated with flour. In a large skillet, heat half the oil and sauté fish pieces, part at a time, until golden and tender. Transfer to paper towels to absorb excess oil. Add remaining oil to skillet and sauté onions and green peppers until tender but not browned. Stir in parsley and sauté for 1 minute. In a small mortar, crush all the spices, mix well, then turn into the vegetable mixture and sauté for another 2 minutes. Pour in wine and lemon juice. Heat just enough to mix everything well, then turn into a blender or food processor fitted with the steel blade and process to a lumpy puree.

In a narrow, deep glass container similar to a canister, arrange a layer of fish pieces on the bottom, pour on some marinade, drop in a few olives, sprinkle with some of the grated lemon rind, and add a bay leaf. Continue layering for five more layers until all ingredients are used. Cover the container and refrigerate for 24 hours or longer. Serve several pieces of fish on a bed of shredded lettuce and spoon a little of the marinade and olives over.

MAKES 8 SERVINGS AS A FIRST COURSE OR SALAD.

1974
CINZANO
CINZANO
Schwarze
Katz
1977
BLUE NUN
RESERVE DE L'ABBÉ
RUFFINO
Pinot Chardonnay Mâcon
1977

RED SNAPPER WITH YOGURT AND CUCUMBER

1½ pounds boned red snapper fillets
one 3-ounce onion, minced
1 cup chopped cucumber, drained
½ teaspoon crushed coriander berries
½ teaspoon grated fresh gingerroot
2 cups plain yogurt
1 cup raw sesame seeds
½ cup mustard or sesame or walnut oil

Cut red snapper into 1-by-2-inch pieces and put into a glass or pottery bowl. Stir onion, cucumber, and spices into yogurt and pour mixture over fish. Let fish marinate for 1 hour, stirring occasionally from top to bottom. While fish is marinating, make Egyptian Rice Pilaf for Fish and keep hot. Lift fish pieces out of marinade, shake off, and roll pieces in sesame seeds. In a large skillet, heat oil until very hot, then sauté the fish pieces over high heat for 1 minute on each side, or until sesame seeds are golden. Transfer fish to a plate and sprinkle with salt. Drain oil from skillet. Spoon in marinade. Simmer over low heat for a few minutes, or until onion and cucumber pieces are tender (yogurt will separate). Pour mixture into blender or food processor, and puree. Return sauce and fish pieces to skillet and heat through. Prepare pilaf. Unmold onto a deep, round plate and arrange red snapper pieces and sauce around it.

MAKES 6 SERVINGS.

Egyptian Rice Pilaf for Fish

In a deep saucepan, heat ¼ cup mustard or sesame or walnut oil and sauté ½ cup slivered blanched almonds or whole pine nuts over medium heat until golden. Lift them out with a skimmer and set aside. Now sauté ½ pound onions, chopped, and 1 chopped green pepper in the oil, stirring often, until onions are translucent. Add 2 cups raw rice and cook, stirring, until kernels turn white. While rice is cooking in oil, stir 1½ teaspoons salt and 1½ teaspoons whole Egyptian saffron into water or stock (adjust salt if stock is already salted). Pour 4½ cups water or fish stock into rice and bring to a boil. Stir to mix well, then reduce to a simmer and cook for 15 to 20 minutes, or until rice is tender and nearly all the liquid is absorbed. Stir in sautéed nuts and 3 tablespoons currants. Cook for 1 minute longer. Firmly press the pilaf into a 6-cup ring mold coated with nonstick surface. Bake in a preheated 400°F. oven for 15 minutes.

MAKES ABOUT 6 CUPS.

CATFISH AND HUSH PUPPIES

six ¾-pound pan-dressed catfish,
skinned (fresh or frozen)
2 tablespoons lemon juice
2 eggs, beaten
2 tablespoons milk
1 teaspoon salt
dash of freshly ground pepper
2 cups dry bread crumbs
fat for deep frying
Hush Puppies (recipe follows)

Thaw fish if frozen. Sprinkle with lemon juice and let stand for 15 minutes. In a shallow bowl, combine eggs, milk, salt, and pepper. Dip fish into egg mixture and roll in bread crumbs. Fry in deep fat heated to 350°F. for 4 to 6 minutes, or until fish is golden brown and flakes easily when tested with a fork. Drain on absorbent paper. Serve with Hush Puppies.

MAKES 6 SERVINGS.

Hush Puppies

1½ cups white cornmeal
½ cup sifted flour
2½ teaspoons baking powder
1 teaspoon salt
¼ teaspoon freshly ground pepper
⅓ cup finely chopped onion
½ cup milk
1 egg, beaten
3 tablespoons oil
fat for deep frying

Sift dry ingredients together. Add remaining ingredients and stir only until blended. Drop by tablespoonfuls into deep fat heated to 350°F., and fry for 2 to 3 minutes, or until golden brown. Drain on absorbent paper.

MAKES 18 HUSH PUPPIES.

FRENCH-QUARTER CATFISH WITH BÉARNAISE SAUCE

six ¾-pound pan-dressed catfish,
skinned (fresh or frozen)
¾ cup French dressing
2 cups fine dry bread crumbs
1 tablespoon butter or
margarine, melted
1½ teaspoons fines herbes
1½ teaspoons paprika
1 teaspoon instant minced onion
¾ teaspoon salt
½ teaspoon celery salt

Thaw fish if frozen. Wash and dry fish. Brush fish inside and outside with French dressing; arrange in a shallow dish. Refrigerate, covered, for 1 to 2 hours, brushing French dressing over fish several times.

In a large bowl, combine bread crumbs, butter or margarine, fines herbes, paprika, onion, salt, and celery salt; mix. Roll fish in crumb mixture, then arrange on a well-oiled shallow baking pan. Bake in a preheated 350°F. oven for 30 to 35 minutes, or until fish flakes easily when tested with a fork. While fish is baking, make Béarnaise Sauce (recipe follows) and keep warm. Serve with sauce and wild rice, garnish with avocado and lemon slices, if desired.

MAKES 6 SERVINGS.

Béarnaise Sauce

4 egg yolks
juice of 1 lemon
2 cups (4 sticks) butter, melted
salt and freshly ground pepper to taste
2 tablespoons capers, drained
¼ cup chopped fresh parsley
1 tablespoon tarragon vinegar

In the top part of a double boiler, beat egg yolks and lemon juice. Set top pan over bottom pan filled with hot water, and cook slowly, never allowing water in the bottom pan to come to a boil. Slowly add melted butter to egg yolks, stirring constantly with a wooden spoon. Add salt and pepper, capers, parsley, and vinegar.

MAKES ABOUT 3 CUPS.

COD PUDDING

1½ pounds fresh cod, skinned and boned
1 tablespoon butter, softened
2 tablespoons dry bread crumbs
½ cup light cream
1 cup heavy cream
2 teaspoons salt
4 teaspoons corn flour

Coat the inside of a 4-cup mold with the softened butter and sprinkle with bread crumbs. Tip the mold from side to side to spread the crumbs evenly. Tap out any excess crumbs. Mix light and heavy cream together. In a blender, puree the cod with a small amount of cream; continue adding cream until you have a smooth blend. Place the pureed mixture in a large bowl and add the salt and corn flour. Beat vigorously until light and fluffy. Pour the puree into the mold. Gently shake and tap the mold sharply to remove any air pockets. Cover the mold with a sheet of buttered aluminum foil and set in a baking dish with sides deep enough to hold a water level three-quarters of the height of the mold. Place in the middle of a 350°F. preheated oven, and bake for 1 to 1¼ hours. Check occasionally, making certain the water is just simmering (if it boils, the molded fish will become perforated). Serve pudding either hot or cold, with or without a suitable sauce, such as lobster, dill, caper, or egg sauce.

MAKES 4 SERVINGS.

NOTE: *Leftovers are good on a bun with chili sauce.*

COD FLORENTINE

2 pounds fresh cod fillets
equal parts water and dry white wine
1 teaspoon salt
2 stems fresh parsley
1 bay leaf
2 pounds fresh spinach, or three
    10-ounce packages frozen
    leaf spinach
1 teaspoon freshly grated nutmeg
6 tablespoons grated Parmesan
    cheese or a mixture of grated
    Parmesan, Romano, and Gruyère

Place the cod fillets in a poacher or skillet, and pour in just enough water and wine to cover fish. Add salt, parsley stems, and bay leaf. Poach for 6 minutes. Remove fillets to a warmed platter. Reduce the broth to half, strain, and reserve it for Mornay Sauce. Steam the spinach but do not overcook; drain, sprinkle with nutmeg, and set aside, but keep warm. Make Mornay Sauce (recipe follows).

Arrange fish fillets over a bed of spinach on a serving platter, or surround the fillets with spinach for easier serving. Cover the fish with sauce and sprinkle lightly with grated cheese. Quickly brown under the broiler.

MAKES 4 TO 6 SERVINGS.

Mornay Sauce

2 cups light cream
½ pound Gruyère cheese, grated (2 cups)
salt to taste
¼ teaspoon cayenne pepper
1 teaspoon freshly ground white pepper
¼ cup butter
¼ cup flour
reserved cod broth

In the top part of a double boiler, combine the cream, cheese, salt, cayenne pepper, and white pepper. In a small skillet or saucepan, make a roux: Melt butter until it foams, stir in flour, and cook for 2 minutes. Scald the cream mixture in the double boiler over steaming water, but do not let it boil. Whip in the roux. Cook for 8 to 10 minutes. Adjust consistency with reserved strained cod broth.

MAKES ABOUT 3 CUPS.

SALT COD AND PEANUT STEW

2 pounds hard salt cod
12 small white onions
1½ pounds fresh plum tomatoes, or 3 cups canned peeled plum tomatoes, chopped
¼ cup olive oil
one 3-ounce yellow onion, minced
2 teaspoons curry powder
1 pound green frying peppers, cut in squares
1 pound yellow summer squash, cut in chunks
½ pound shelled unroasted peanuts
salt to taste
2 cups cooked rice
4 teaspoons grated lemon rind
¼ cup minced fresh parsley

Start the day before you wish to serve by soaking cod in cold water in a glass or ceramic container for 24 hours, changing the water three times.

Next day, drain cod and transfer to a poacher or very large, deep skillet. Cover with fresh cold water, bring to a boil, and simmer for 10 minutes. Strain and reserve poaching liquid. Turn cod pieces out onto a cloth towel and cut into chunks; remove skin and any bones. Peel white onions and cut a cross in the base of each one. If using fresh tomatoes, blanch, peel, and chop, discarding as many seeds as possible. In a large kettle, heat oil and sauté minced yellow onion until tender. Add curry powder and cook, stirring, until browned. Gently stir in *whole* white onions, peppers, squash, and chopped tomatoes. Pour in 5 cups of the reserved poaching liquid and bring the stew to a boil. Reduce to a simmer and add peanuts. Let stew simmer for 1 hour; if necessary, add more of the reserved poaching liquid. Test the peanuts; they should be tender, like a cooked dried bean, but not mushy; if still hard, cook longer. When peanuts are done, add cod chunks and simmer for 5 minutes. Taste; a little salt may be needed, as peanuts absorb salt. Put a large scoop of rice into the center of each of six to eight large, deep soup plates. Spoon some vegetables and cod into each plate and ladle broth over all. Sprinkle with lemon rind and parsley.

MAKES 6 TO 8 SERVINGS.

NOTE: *This recipe was adapted from a West African vegetable stew. It is quite pungent. If you prefer a milder taste, use less curry powder.*

BAKED HADDOCK WITH LOBSTER SAUCE

four 8- to 10-ounce fillets of haddock, skinned
Lobster Sauce (recipe follows)
6 tablespoons oil
3 cups fine unseasoned bread crumbs
garnish: cooked lobster meat

Make Lobster Sauce and keep warm. Dip haddock fillets into oil and then into bread crumbs to coat them generously. (There will be oil and crumbs left over.) Place breaded fillets on an oiled baking sheet and bake in a preheated 425°F. oven for 10 minutes, or until browned. Arrange fillets on a warmed serving platter. Spoon Lobster Sauce over fish and garnish with additional chopped lobster meat. Serve with potatoes and green beans.

MAKES 4 SERVINGS.

Lobster Sauce

1/4 cup butter
1 tablespoon finely chopped onion
1 tablespoon minced lobster meat
1 teaspoon paprika
1/4 cup flour
2 cups light cream
1/4 teaspoon salt
1/4 teaspoon freshly ground white pepper
sherry to taste
1/4 cup coarsely chopped lobster meat

In a saucepan, melt butter and sauté onion for 2 minutes over medium heat. Add minced lobster meat and sauté for 2 more minutes. Add paprika, stir, and remove from heat. Add flour, then cook over low heat, stirring, for 2 minutes. Stir in cream, seasonings, and sherry. Simmer until thickened. Stir in chopped lobster meat.

MAKES ABOUT 2 CUPS.

TOURNEDOS OF CANADIAN LOTTE WITH NOODLES

four ½-inch-thick lotte steaks
salt and freshly ground pepper
flour for dredging
¼ pound (1 stick) butter
1 shallot, minced
1 cup dry white wine
½ teaspoon whole saffron
1 bay leaf
2 cups heavy cream
2 cups cooked medium-width noodles, hot
garnish: 1 tomato, blanched, seeded, and diced

Season lotte steaks with salt and pepper; dredge with flour and shake off excess. In a very large skillet, melt half the butter. Sauté steaks on one side for 5 minutes; turn over and sauté on the other side for 5 minutes. Remove fish from pan and keep warm. In a saucepan, melt the remaining butter and sauté shallot until soft. Add wine and cook over low heat until liquid is reduced to half. Stir in half the saffron, the bay leaf, and the cream. Cook cream mixture over low heat, reducing it slowly until it is heavy enough to coat the fish. Strain cream mixture and stir in remaining saffron. Place noodles on a serving platter. Arrange lotte steaks on the bed of noodles. Cover with cream sauce and sprinkle diced tomato on top.

MAKES 4 SERVINGS.

NOTE: *Lotte is a restaurant name for the goosefish, also known as monkfish or anglerfish.*

NEW ENGLAND FISH CHOWDER

2 pounds haddock, cod, tautog,
rockfish, or black bass fillets
2 pounds potatoes, peeled
2 quarts milk
½ pound lean salt pork, diced
2 pounds onions, sliced in rings
salt and freshly ground white
pepper to taste
1 bay leaf
1 teaspoon dried thyme
6 pats butter

In a 4-quart kettle, boil potatoes; drain and set aside to cool. Pour milk into kettle set over very low heat. In a skillet, sauté salt pork until crisp and browned. Remove cubes with a spatula or slotted spoon and add to the milk. Leave rendered fat in skillet. Sauté onion rings in skillet until translucent but not browned; remove and add to kettle. Place fish fillets in skillet with fat that remains, cover, and simmer until the fish flakes easily; add fish to kettle. Dice the potatoes and add to soup mixture. Season with salt and pepper. Add bay leaf and thyme. Simmer for 15 minutes. Serve each portion in a bowl with a pat of butter floating on top. Accompany with ship's biscuits.

MAKES 6 SERVINGS.

COLD FISH WITH PARSLEY SAUCE

3 thick 1-pound codfish steaks
3 tablespoons olive oil
1 large leek, thinly sliced
one 3-ounce onion, chopped
¼ cup celery leaves
1 bunch fresh parsley, stems
separated from leaves
salt and freshly ground white pepper
1½ cups dry white wine (French
Colombard or Green Hungarian)
½ cup mayonnaise
½ cup plain yogurt or sour cream
lemon juice (optional)
garnish: 6 strips pimiento or lemon rind

Rinse fish steaks and pat dry. Heat oil in a skillet or other pan large enough to hold fish steaks in a single layer. Add leek, onion, celery leaves, and parsley stems. Sauté, stirring often, until onion and leek are translucent. Remove pan from heat and carefully arrange steaks on top of vegetables. Sprinkle fish lightly with salt and white pepper. Pour wine around the fish, and, if necessary, add enough water to reach top of steaks (amount depends on size and shape of pan). Measure a sheet of aluminum foil large enough to cover the pan, and press over the fish, making a small hole in the center for steam to escape. Bring to a boil (steam will rise from the center hole), then at once reduce to a gentle simmer; cover with skillet lid. Simmer steaks for 5 to 10 minutes, depending on the thickness of the pieces. With a slotted pancake turner, carefully remove steaks to a platter and let cool. Pour cooking liquid through a fine sieve and let it cool. Remove skin, bones, and any fatty sections from fish steaks and arrange on serving platter.

Place parsley leaves in food processor fitted with the steel blade and mince. Add mayonnaise, yogurt or sour cream, and ½ cup cooking liquid; mix. Add more of the cooking liquid as needed to give the sauce the texture of a thin mayonnaise. Adjust seasoning to taste. If sauce is not tart enough, add a little lemon juice. Spoon sauce over fish and garnish each steak with a strip of pimiento or lemon rind. Serve cold or at cool room temperature and accompany with rice or tabbouli salad.

MAKES 6 SERVINGS, OR 12 SERVINGS AS A FIRST COURSE.

NOTE: *Smaller fish steaks may be prepared in the same way. Salmon looks particularly pretty with this green sauce.*

RED DRUM CUSTARD

1½ pounds red drum fillets, skinned and cut into 1-inch-wide strips
2 tablespoons butter
¼ cup chopped fresh parsley
½ cup finely chopped celery with leaves
1 small onion, chopped
3 cups soft bread crumbs
1 quart milk
4 eggs
2 teaspoons salt
¼ teaspoon freshly ground pepper
½ pound sharp Cheddar cheese, grated (2 cups)
⅓ cup chopped pimiento
garnish: red and green pepper

In a large skillet, heat butter and sauté parsley, celery, and onion for 5 minutes. Add fillets and continue cooking for 5 minutes. Remove from heat and let cool. In a bowl, mix bread crumbs with milk and eggs, then beat until well blended. Stir in salt, pepper, and contents of skillet. Fold in half the cheese and the pimiento. Pour mixture into an 8-by-8-by-2-inch greased baking pan. Sprinkle with remaining cheese. Bake in a preheated 350°F. oven for 40 to 45 minutes, or until custard is lightly browned and firm to the touch at the center. Garnish with red and green pepper rings.

MAKES 4 SERVINGS, OR 6 SERVINGS AS A FIRST COURSE.

RED DRUM AND MUSHROOM PIE

1½ pounds red drum fillets, skinned
    and cut into 1-inch-wide strips
pastry for single-crust 9-inch pie
6 ounces Gruyère cheese, grated
    (1½ cups)
flour
2 tablespoons butter
2 cups sliced fresh mushrooms, or
    one 6-ounce can sliced
    mushrooms, drained
4 eggs
2 cups half-and-half
¼ teaspoon dried oregano
¼ teaspoon dried thyme
½ teaspoon salt
garnish: fresh or dried oregano,
    tiny fresh mushrooms

Lay pastry in a 9-inch pie pan and flute the edge. Mix the cheese and flour and spread evenly in the bottom of the unbaked pastry. In a skillet, melt butter and sauté fish fillets for about 5 minutes. Place the fish and mushrooms in the pastry. In a bowl, beat the eggs with the half-and-half, herbs, and salt. Pour this mixture over the fish and mushrooms. Bake in a preheated oven at 350°F. for 45 minutes, or until pie is puffed and browned. Cool for 10 minutes before cutting into wedges.

Serve garnished with a sprig of fresh oregano, or a sprinkling of dried oregano, and tiny whole mushrooms.

MAKES 6 LUNCH SERVINGS.

NOTE: *The red drum is commonly marketed as "redfish" in the southern United States.*

SPOTS EN PAPILLOTE

- four ½-pound Virginia spots, whole-dressed
- olive oil
- 2 tablespoons butter
- 6 ounces fresh mushrooms, chopped
- 1 small onion, chopped
- 2 tablespoons minced fresh curly parsley
- 2 slices whole wheat bread, cubed
- ¼ cup tomato puree
- ¼ cup dry white wine
- 1 teaspoon salt
- ¼ teaspoon ground coriander
- 2 teaspoons Dijon mustard

Rinse fish and pat dry. Cut four 12-by-16-inch sheets of heavy-duty aluminum foil, fold each in half, and cut into the shape of a folded heart. Unfold and brush one side of the heart with oil; set aside. In a skillet, melt butter and sauté mushrooms and onion until limp. Add parsley and continue to sauté for a few minutes. Add the bread cubes, tomato puree, half the wine, the salt, coriander, and half the mustard; mix and remove from heat. In a bowl, mix remaining wine and mustard and brush the fish with the mixture on both sides. Divide the stuffing mixture among the fish. If there is any left, pat it around the tail portions of the fish. Wrap each fish in a piece of foil and crimp the edges. Place packages on a baking sheet and bake in a preheated 375°F. oven for 30 minutes. Test one package; if not done, bake for a few minutes longer. Serve in the packages, to be opened at table.

MAKES 4 SERVINGS.

NOTE: *Market-identified with Virginia, the spot occurs from Cape Cod to Mexico. It is known as "Lafayette" in the New York area.*

STIR-FRIED CROAKER

2 pounds croaker fillets or other fish fillets (fresh or frozen)
2 tablespoons soy sauce
2 tablespoons dry sherry
1/4 teaspoon sugar
1/4 teaspoon cayenne pepper
1/8 teaspoon ground ginger
1/2 cup oil
1 cup raw cashews
4 cups sliced unpeeled zucchini
4 cups sliced fresh mushrooms
4 cups diagonally sliced bok choy
2 cups fresh snow peas
16 whole green onions, cut into 3-inch pieces (2 cups)
1/2 teaspoon salt

Thaw fish if frozen. Skin fillets, and cut them into 2-inch cubes. In 1½-quart bowl, combine soy sauce, sherry, sugar, cayenne pepper, and ginger; mix well. Add fish and stir. Marinate in refrigerator for 15 minutes.

In a 12-inch skillet or wok, heat oil over medium-high heat. Add cashews and cook, stirring constantly, for about 3 minutes, or until lightly browned. Remove cashews with slotted spoon and place on absorbent paper. Add zucchini, mushrooms, bok choy, snow peas, green onions, and salt to remaining oil and cook, stirring constantly, over medium heat until tender-crisp, about 5 minutes. With slotted spoon, remove vegetables from pan to a large bowl; set aside. Add fish to skillet, reduce heat, and cover. Cook fish over low heat for 8 to 10 minutes, or until fish flakes easily when tested with a fork. Add cashews and cooked vegetables to fish in skillet. Stir carefully. Heat for 1 to 2 minutes before serving. Serve immediately.

MAKES 6 SERVINGS.

TRIPLE TREAT

1½ pounds croaker fillets or other fish fillets (fresh or frozen)
6 medium ripe tomatoes
¼ cup butter or margarine, softened
1 tablespoon minced fresh parsley
1 tablespoon lemon juice
½ teaspoon Worcestershire sauce
½ teaspoon grated onion
½ teaspoon salt
⅛ teaspoon liquid hot pepper sauce
½ cup coarsely grated sharp Cheddar cheese
3 cups mashed potatoes, seasoned
1 egg yolk
garnish: fresh parsley

Thaw fillets if frozen. Skin fillets, and divide into six equal portions. Cut a slice off the top of each tomato and scoop out center. Set tomatoes upside down to drain. In a bowl, combine butter or margarine, parsley, lemon juice, Worcestershire sauce, onion, salt, and liquid hot pepper sauce; set aside. Roll each fillet turban-style and secure with a wooden food pick. Stand turbans on end in a well-greased 8-inch-square baking dish. Top each turban with some of the grated cheese. Bake in a preheated 350°F. oven for 10 to 12 minutes. Remove food picks and place a turban inside each tomato cup. Place the stuffed tomatoes in the center of a well-greased 12-by-8-by-2-inch baking dish. Spoon approximately 2 teaspoons of the seasoned butter mixture into each tomato cup. Pipe mashed potatoes through pastry tube into the base of each tomato. Brush potatoes with egg yolk. Bake in the 350°F. oven for 12 to 15 minutes, or until tomatoes are done and fish flakes easily when tested with a fork. Garnish with chopped parsley.

MAKES 6 SERVINGS.

CATCH-OF-THE-DAY STEW

2 to 3 pounds fish fillets, cut into chunks
2 tablespoons olive oil
2 tablespoons butter
2 tablespoons minced fresh parsley
3 medium onions, sliced
1 tablespoon minced fresh basil, or 1 teaspoon dried basil
¼ teaspoon ground saffron
2 bay leaves
pinch of crushed red pepper
2 cloves garlic, pressed (or more according to taste)
2 cups coarsely chopped fresh Italian plum tomatoes
1 cup tomato puree
½ cup dry white wine
salt and freshly ground pepper to taste
½ cup Greek olives, pitted and halved

In a large skillet or stewpot, heat olive oil and butter. Sauté parsley, onions, herbs, and crushed red pepper over medium heat until onions are wilted. Add garlic and sauté a bit longer. Add tomatoes, tomato puree, wine, and salt and pepper. Simmer to blend flavors. Add fish chunks and olives. Continue cooking over low heat until fish is *al dente.* Taste for seasoning. Serve over toast or crisp fried bread, or accompany with crisp French bread.

MAKES 4 SERVINGS.

NOTE: *Don't hesitate to add fresh clams or mussels if these are available at the seashore.*

PETRALE SOLE EN PAPILLOTE

one ½-pound fillet of petrale sole
2 tablespoons butter
6 medium fresh mushrooms, finely chopped
1 teaspoon chopped shallot
¼ cup dry vermouth
½ teaspoon chopped fresh parsley
oil
salt and freshly ground pepper
3 thin slices lemon
garnish: ripe tomato and fresh parsley

In a skillet, melt the butter and sauté mushrooms and shallot until tender. Add vermouth and, over low heat, reduce until liquid is almost entirely evaporated. Puree mixture in a blender or food processor. Mix in parsley and set aside.

For the *papillote,* use Patapar (parchment paper) and oil; if Patapar is not available, substitute brown wrapping paper. (When using brown paper, line a shallow baking pan with aluminum foil to keep paper from burning and smoking; oil paper lightly to prevent sticking.) Be sure to cut off sufficient quantities of either Patapar or brown paper for folding and crimping to close.

Cut a sheet of parchment paper to the size of a large dinner plate and oil it lightly. Place mushroom puree on one half of the paper. Lightly salt and pepper the fish and arrange it on the puree. Garnish with lemon slices. Fold the parchment over in *papillote* fashion and crimp edges together. Bake in a preheated 375°F. oven for 20 minutes. Place on a serving plate garnished with tomato slices and parsley sprigs.

MAKES 1 SERVING.

HALIBUT FILLETS IN LETTUCE LEAVES

four ½-pound fillets of halibut
1 cup dry white wine
14 to 16 lettuce leaves
salt and freshly ground pepper
2 small leeks, white parts only, cut into crosswise slices
2 small carrots, cut into crosswise slices
approximately 1 cup fish stock
2 tablespoons pureed cooked mushrooms
2 tablespoons cottage cheese

Marinate halibut in wine for 15 minutes. Remove fish, and reserve the wine. Spread lettuce leaves on work surface and arrange fish on top. Sprinkle fish with salt and pepper and scatter leek and carrot slices on top. Wrap lettuce around fillets and vegetables, making four individual packages. Place packages in a buttered shallow baking pan. Pour reserved wine around fish and add enough stock to cover fish. Simmer, covered, over low heat for 15 minutes. Remove packages from pan but keep them warm. Reduce cooking liquid to about ½ cup. Blend in mushroom puree and cottage cheese, and keep sauce warm without boiling. Arrange fish packages on serving platter, with carrots and leeks. Serve sauce separately.

MAKES 4 SERVINGS.

FILLET OF FLOUNDER MARGUERY

six 1/4-pound fillets of flounder
equal parts water and dry white
wine to cover fish
1 bay leaf
2 stems fresh parsley
salt to taste
6 large fresh shrimps, butterflied
24 mussels
2 cups Mornay sauce (see p. 73)
garnish: fresh parsley

Starting with the tail end, roll up each flounder fillet. Cut each roll in half, to make twelve small *paupiettes.* (These small rolls are much easier to serve.) In a fish poacher or deep baking pan, combine water, wine, bay leaf, parsley stems, and salt. Poach the rolled fillets for 6 to 8 minutes, or until they are translucent but still firm. Arrange the fillets on a heatproof serving platter and keep warm. Poach the shrimps in the same broth; remove shrimps and reserve broth. In a saucepan, steam the mussels in a small amount of water for 5 minutes, or until the shells open. Drain and separate mussel meats from shells; reserve shells. Adjust consistency of the Mornay sauce with the fish broth. Top fillets with the sauce and brown under the broiler. Garnish with mussel meats, shrimps, and mussel shells (as shown). Sprinkle with chopped parsley.

MAKES 6 SERVINGS.

FLOUNDER APPLEDORE

- four 1-pound flounders, dressed
- 1/4 pound (1 stick) butter
- 1/2 cup chopped celery
- 1/4 cup chopped onion
- 1/2 cup crab meat
- 4 cups soft bread crumbs
- 3 tablespoons prepared mustard
- 1 egg, beaten
- 1 teaspoon ground dried thyme
- 1 teaspoon salt
- 1 teaspoon freshly ground white pepper
- lemon juice

With a sharp-pointed, thin-bladed knife, make a 6-to-8-inch-long slit along the white side of the flounder. This cut should be above and to the backbone. Lay the knife flat and slide it along the backbone, cutting each side to create a large pocket (this bone must remain in thin-bodied flatfish). Do not penetrate the body cavity.

In a skillet, melt the butter and sauté celery and onion for 2 minutes. Add crab meat and sauté for another 2 minutes. In a large bowl, combine bread crumbs, sautéed mixture, mustard, egg, thyme, salt, and pepper. Mix thoroughly, moistening the stuffing with lemon juice. Stuff the pocket in each flounder. Place the fish on a baking pan with about 1/2 inch of water to create steam. Bake in a preheated 425°F. oven for 15 to 20 minutes.

MAKES 4 SERVINGS.

SCANDINAVIAN-STYLE PERCH WITH SHRIMP STUFFING

two 2-pound yellow perch, dressed
salt and freshly ground pepper
1 pound raw shrimps, shelled and
deveined
⅓ cup butter, melted
½ teaspoon paprika
¼ cup lemon juice
½ cup seasoned dry bread crumbs
2 tablespoons butter
2 tablespoons flour
1 cup half-and-half
2 tablespoons snipped fresh chives
garnish: dill

Sprinkle perch inside and out with salt and pepper. With a sharp knife, slash each perch lengthwise down the center of the fish. With the tip of the knife, shape a pocket by running the knife lengthwise under both sides of the first slash, along the rib bones and the backbone. Open out perch. In a medium-size bowl, combine shrimps, the ⅓ cup melted butter, the paprika, lemon juice, and bread crumbs. Use mixture to stuff perch. Place perch on a buttered shallow baking pan. Bake in a preheated 350°F. oven for 25 to 30 minutes, or until perch are cooked.

To prepare sauce, melt the 2 tablespoons butter in a small saucepan and stir in flour. Gradually stir in half-and-half and chives. Cook, stirring, over medium heat until sauce thickens and bubbles. Season with salt and pepper to taste.

Place perch on a warmed serving platter and spoon sauce over fish. Serve with cooked new potatoes sautéed in butter with chopped fresh dill. Garnish with fresh dill sprigs.

MAKES 4 SERVINGS.

SMOKED FISH LOGS

2 cups flaked smoked mullet, or
other hot smoked fish
8 ounces cream cheese, softened
1 tablespoon lemon juice
1 tablespoon minced onion
1 tablespoon prepared horseradish
¼ teaspoon salt
½ cup finely chopped pecans
2 tablespoons chopped parsley

To make logs, the fish must have a full smoke flavor. Cold smoked fish will be too bland for this hors d'oeuvre. Species that are generally hot smoked such as mullet, Spanish mackerel, king mackerel, cod, bluefish, or striped bass make the best logs.

Combine cheese, lemon juice, onion, horseradish (add more if you like), salt, and fish; mix thoroughly. Shape fish mixture into small logs. Chill for several hours. Combine pecans and parsley. Roll fish logs in nut mixture. Serve with assorted crackers.

MAKES 24 TO 36 LOGS.

MULLET TURBANS WITH LEMON-RICE STUFFING

12 fillets of mullet, skinned
Lemon-Rice Stuffing (recipe follows)
1 teaspoon salt

Make Lemon-Rice Stuffing. Using two fillets for each portion, roll paired fillets (tail end to head end) to form a turban and secure with food picks. Stand turbans on end in a shallow baking dish. Sprinkle salt evenly over fish. Spoon ¾ cup stuffing inside each fish portion. Bake in a preheated 350°F. oven for 25 to 30 minutes. Remove food picks before serving.

MAKES 6 SERVINGS.

Lemon-Rice Stuffing

¼ cup melted fat or oil
¾ cup chopped celery
½ cup chopped onion
1⅓ cups water
2 tablespoons grated lemon rind
1 teaspoon paprika
1 teaspoon salt
pinch of dried thyme
1½ cups cooked rice
⅓ cup sour cream
¼ cup diced peeled lemon

In a saucepan, heat fat or oil and sauté celery and onion until tender. Add water, lemon rind, paprika, salt, and thyme; bring to a boil. Add rice and stir to moisten. Cover and remove from heat. Let stand for 5 to 10 minutes, or until liquid is absorbed. Add sour cream and lemon; mix thoroughly.

MAKES ABOUT 4½ CUPS.

FRIED MULLET WITH MACADAMIA NUT SAUCE

2 pounds mullet fillets, skinned
1 cup buttermilk
1 cup buttermilk biscuit mix
2 teaspoons salt
fat or oil for frying
Macadamia Nut Sauce (recipe follows)

Cut fillets into serving-size portions. Place mullet in a single layer in a shallow pan. Pour the buttermilk over the fish and let stand for 30 minutes, turning once.

Combine biscuit mix and salt. Remove mullet from buttermilk and roll in biscuit mix. Panfry fish in 1 inch of hot fat (not smoking) for 3 to 4 minutes, turning once. Drain on absorbent paper. Serve with Macadamia Nut Sauce.

MAKES 6 SERVINGS.

Macadamia Nut Sauce

¼ pound (1 stick) butter or margarine, melted
1 cup macadamia nuts, coarsely chopped
1 tablespoon chopped fresh parsley

In a skillet, melt butter or margarine and brown nuts. Add parsley and stir.

MAKES 1 CUP.

POACHED WOLFFISH WITH SHRIMP-CURRY SAUCE

2 pounds wolffish fillets
Shrimp-Curry Sauce (recipe follows)
1 teaspoon salt
½ teaspoon freshly ground pepper
1 bay leaf
1 slice onion

Make Shrimp-Curry Sauce and keep warm. Wrap fillets in cheesecloth and place in boiling water. To the water add salt, pepper, bay leaf, and onion. Simmer for 10 to 16 minutes, or until fish is white throughout and soft to the touch; drain. Serve with sauce.

MAKES 6 SERVINGS.

Shrimp-Curry Sauce

2 cups water
¼ teaspoon dried thyme
¼ teaspoon lemon juice
¼ onion
1 tablespoon minced celery leaves
1 bay leaf
½ cup small raw shrimps, shelled and deveined
2 tablespoons butter
2 tablespoons flour
1 cup light cream
1 teaspoon curry powder

In a small pan, bring the water to a boil. Season with thyme, lemon juice, onion, celery leaves, and bay leaf. Add shrimps and simmer for 10 minutes. Remove shrimps from liquid and cool them. Strain cooking liquid and reserve. Mince shrimps and set aside. In the top part of a double boiler, melt the butter, stir in the flour, and cook over low heat until blended in a roux. To the roux add 1 cup of the reserved cooking liquid and the cream. Set the top pan over boiling water and simmer the sauce for 15 minutes. Just before serving add the curry powder and minced shrimps.

MAKES ABOUT 2 CUPS.

CRISP BROILED KING MACKEREL

2 pounds king mackerel steaks or
other fish steaks
¼ pound (1 stick) butter or
margarine, melted
¼ cup lemon juice
1 teaspoon salt
1 clove garlic, minced
dash of paprika
1 cup crushed potato chips
½ cup crushed saltines
garnish: lemon

Cut steaks into serving-size portions. Place fish in a shallow baking dish. In a bowl, combine butter or margarine, lemon juice, salt, garlic, and paprika. Pour mixture over fish and marinate for 30 minutes, turning once.

Remove fish from marinade. Reserve the marinade. Combine crushed potato chips and saltines. Roll fish in crumb mixture. Place fish on a well-greased broiler pan, and drizzle marinade evenly over fish. Broil about 5 inches from source of heat for 5 to 7 minutes, or until browned. Turn carefully and broil for 5 to 7 minutes longer, or until top is browned and fish flakes easily when tested with a fork. Serve with lemon wedges.

MAKES 6 SERVINGS.

PATRICK'S POMPANO

4 small fillets of pompano
Dill Sauce (recipe follows)
3 tablespoons butter, softened
1 tablespoon snipped fresh dill
3 tablespoons minced fresh parsley
melted butter
1 shallot, minced
pinch of salt

Make Dill Sauce and keep warm. Coat a shallow baking dish with the 3 tablespoons butter and the dill. Arrange pompano fillets in the dish. Mix parsley, melted butter, shallot, and salt together and pour over fish. Cover the dish tightly with aluminum foil and set on a rack over boiling water in a low roasting pan. Steam the fish on top of the stove until the flesh is white and firm, about 6 to 8 minutes. Remove foil and serve in the same dish. Pour Dill Sauce over the pompano.

MAKES 4 SERVINGS.

Dill Sauce

3 tablespoons butter
3 tablespoons flour
½ cup fish stock or clam juice
1 cup light cream
½ cup dry vermouth
½ cup chopped fresh parsley
¾ cup snipped fresh dill
salt and freshly ground white pepper to taste

In a skillet, melt the butter, stir in the flour, and cook over low heat until blended into a roux. Add fish stock or clam juice, cream, vermouth, parsley, and dill. Stir over low heat until thickened and smooth. Season with salt and pepper.

MAKES ABOUT 3 CUPS.

BAKED POMPANO WITH ORANGE-BUTTER SAUCE

two 2- to 3-pound pompano, dressed
¼ cup butter, melted
Orange-Butter Sauce (recipe follows)
garnish: orange slices

Brush pompano with melted butter and bake in a preheated 350°F. oven for 35 to 40 minutes. Butter-baste the fish until golden brown. Meanwhile make Orange-Butter Sauce and keep warm. When fish is ready, arrange on a serving dish and cover with sauce. Garnish with orange slices. Serve with carrots and boiled new potatoes.

MAKES 4 SERVINGS.

Orange-Butter Sauce

one 6-ounce can frozen orange juice concentrate
¼ cup lemon juice
½ teaspoon dry mustard
¼ teaspoon crumbled dried rosemary
½ teaspoon celery salt
½ teaspoon onion powder
½ teaspoon salt
¼ teaspoon Angostura bitters
¼ pound (1 stick) butter or margarine

In a heavy saucepan, combine all ingredients except butter or margarine. Heat slowly, stirring constantly, until mixture comes to a boil; boil for 1 minute. Add butter or margarine and stir until melted and combined.

MAKES ABOUT 1 CUP.

ESCABECHE

6 pounds firm-fleshed fish
(mackerel, tuna, pompano, bass)
1/4 cup salt
1 quart water
6 to 8 tablespoons olive oil
2 large cloves garlic, minced
2 red bell peppers, minced
1 large bay leaf
juice of 1 large lime
1 red chili pepper, thinly sliced
1 large red onion, thinly sliced
1/2 cup white wine vinegar
2 teaspoons minced fresh oregano,
or 3/4 teaspoon dried oregano
2 teaspoons sweet marjoram, or
3/4 teaspoon dried marjoram
1/4 teaspoon ground cuminseed
3 drops Tabasco
chicken stock or chicken broth
or water
garnish: lettuce or watercress, black
Spanish or Mediterranean-type
olives, tomatoes, hard-cooked eggs

Cut fish into bite-size chunks. Make a salt solution with the salt and water, and marinate fish in this for about 30 minutes; drain and pat dry. In a very large, heavy skillet, heat about 6 tablespoons oil; briefly sauté garlic. Add red peppers, bay leaf, and fish, in several batches, if necessary; sauté for about 15 minutes, turning once. Remove to a bowl, sprinkle with lime juice, and set aside.

Add 1 or 2 tablespoons more oil to skillet; sauté chili pepper and onion until onion is translucent. Add vinegar, oregano, marjoram, cuminseed, and Tabasco. Simmer slowly for about 15 minutes, adding 1 tablespoon chicken stock or chicken broth or water if liquid cooks away; add more if needed, 1 tablespoon at a time. Remove from heat; let cool.

Pour sauce over fish and carefully but thoroughly mix with a wooden spoon. Refrigerate or keep in a cool place, depending on length of waiting time, until ready to serve. Serve on bed of lettuce or watercress with ripe olives and tomato and hard-cooked-egg wedges. Accompany with chilled fino sherry or cream sherry on the rocks.

MAKES 6 SERVINGS.

MOUSSE OF SALMON AND PETRALE SOLE

1 pound boned salmon
1 pound boned petrale sole
1 teaspoon salt
½ teaspoon freshly ground pepper
2 egg whites
½ pound (2 sticks) butter, melted
and cooled
4 slices truffles, chopped
4 fresh mushroom caps, chopped
1 tablespoon chopped fresh chives
½ cup shelled pistachio nuts

Grind salmon and sole into a large bowl. Add all other ingredients except mayonnaise and mix well in a blender or food processor. Transfer to a well-buttered 6-cup terrine. Bake, covered, in a preheated 325°F. oven for 45 minutes. Let cool, then refrigerate for 2 hours. Make Herb-Flavored Mayonnaise and serve with fish.

MAKES 6 TO 8 SERVINGS AS A FIRST COURSE.

Herb-Flavored Mayonnaise

1 egg yolk
pinch of salt
pinch of freshly ground pepper
1 teaspoon lemon juice
1 teaspoon minced fresh chives
1 teaspoon minced watercress
1 teaspoon minced fresh parsley
1 tablespoon olive oil
½ cup cottage cheese

In a medium bowl, combine the egg yolk, salt, pepper, lemon juice, and herbs. Beat with a whisk, egg beater, or blender until well mixed. Then add oil, drop by drop, mixing continuously, until mixture thickens. Slowly add cottage cheese until well blended.

MAKES ABOUT 1½ CUPS.

BAKED SALMON WITH ASPARAGUS

four 6-ounce slices boned salmon
½ pound boned sole
1 cup heavy cream
12 fresh asparagus tips, cooked
4 pork fat nets (pig's caul)
1 cup dry white wine
4 teaspoons minced shallots

Lay salmon slices out flat. Make sole puree: grind sole, then puree with half the cream in a blender or food processor. Spread half the puree in the center of the salmon slices, arrange three asparagus tips on top of each slice, and spread remaining puree on top of asparagus. Roll each salmon slice around the puree and asparagus into the shape of a small salami. Wrap each package in pork fat net and tie with string.

Pour wine into a skillet with a heatproof handle and add shallots. Arrange salmon rolls on top. Bake, covered, in a preheated 375°F. oven for 15 minutes. Remove salmon rolls from pan, snip strings, and discard pork fat net; keep salmon warm. Set skillet over direct heat and reduce the liquid in it to about half. Stir in remaining ½ cup cream, heat, and pour over salmon.

MAKES 4 SERVINGS.

NOTE: *If pork fat net is difficult to obtain, the salmon rolls may be wrapped in cooking parchment. In that case, increase the wine by ¼ cup.*

CUVEE
CHAMPAGNE
OF FRANCE

SALMON STEAKS WITH SORREL SAUCE

three 1-inch-thick salmon steaks
1 cup champagne
3 shallots, minced
¼ cup butter or margarine
½ cup flour
1 cup heavy cream
½ cup finely chopped cooked sorrel
salt and freshly ground pepper
to taste

Place salmon steaks in a foil-lined and greased shallow baking pan. Pour champagne and shallots over steaks. Bake, covered, in a preheated 350°F. oven for 30 minutes. Drain off 1 cup of the pan juices and reserve for sauce. Drain salmon and keep warm on a serving platter.

In a saucepan, melt butter or margarine and stir in flour. Gradually stir in reserved pan juices and cream. Stir in sorrel. Stir over low heat until sauce thickens and bubbles. Season with salt and pepper. Spoon sauce over salmon steaks, and surround with baby peas.

MAKES 3 SERVINGS.

COULIBIAC OF SALMON

1 pound salmon fillet
3 cups fish stock
1½ cups uncooked rice
salt
1½ pounds puff pastry
½ tablespoon chopped fresh parsley
½ tablespoon chopped fresh dill
pinch of dried oregano
pinch of dried basil
6 tablespoons butter
2 tablespoons finely chopped onion
4 eggs, hard-cooked, shelled,
and sliced
2 eggs, lightly beaten
garnish: sour cream and fresh chives

In a saucepan, bring fish stock to boiling and cook rice until liquid is absorbed; let cool. Poach salmon in lightly salted water until about half-cooked; drain and cool. Roll out pastry to form a 12-by-8-inch rectangle; save all the pastry trimmings. In a small bowl, combine all the herbs together. In a small skillet, melt the butter and sauté onion until golden; set onion aside along with butter. Spread the cooled rice in the center of the pastry. Sprinkle herbs, along with a little salt, over the rice, and place salmon on top. Arrange egg slices over salmon and sprinkle onion with butter over eggs. Fold the long sides of the pastry toward the center over the filling, brush with beaten egg, and pinch to seal. Trim the short ends as necessary, brush with egg, and pinch to seal. Turn the pastry roll seam side down. Roll out all the pastry trimmings, cut into narrow strips, and arrange in a lattice pattern over the top of the *coulibiac*. Brush the entire surface with the remaining beaten egg. Leave in a warm place for 30 minutes, then bake in a preheated 375°F. oven for 30 minutes. Serve with sour cream and chopped chives.

MAKES 4 TO 6 SERVINGS.

WHITEFISH MOUSSE

one 2-pound whitefish, dressed
melted butter
2 envelopes unflavored gelatin
1 cup dry white wine
one $10\frac{1}{2}$-ounce can condensed golden
 mushroom soup
1 cup sour cream
1 cup heavy cream, whipped
salt to taste
6 green peppers or large navel oranges
garnish: green pepper or orange, lettuce,
 lemon, lime

Brush fish with melted butter. Bake in a preheated 350°F. oven for 30 to 35 minutes. Remove from oven and let cool. Remove skin and bones and break fish into bite-size pieces. In a saucepan, mix gelatin and wine. Stir over low heat until gelatin is dissolved. Stir in condensed soup and sour cream. Remove to a large bowl, cover, and chill until slightly thickened. Fold in whitefish and whipped cream. Season with salt. Chill, covered, until firm. Slice tops from peppers and remove seeds, or hollow out oranges. Spoon mousse into peppers or oranges. Chill until ready to serve. Garnish with chopped green pepper or diced orange. Serve on lettuce leaves with lemon and lime slices.

MAKES 6 SERVINGS.

MUSCADET

TROUT FOR POOR YOUNG ANGLERS

- one 2-pound trout, dressed
- 1½ cups fresh orange juice
- ¼ cup fresh lemon juice
- 2 tablespoons olive oil
- 4 cloves garlic
- 6 coriander berries, crushed
- 1 bunch fresh dill
- 1 tablespoon butter
- 12 to 16 shelled walnut halves

Mix orange juice, lemon juice, and oil in a heatproof glass or ceramic baking dish large enough to hold the trout. Peel garlic and drop the whole cloves into the dish. Add coriander and several sprigs of dill. Wipe trout with a damp paper towel and place several sprigs of dill in the fish. Put trout in the marinade and let it soak for about 1 hour, turning fish over several times or spooning marinade over the fish. Remove and discard garlic cloves. Cover dish with aluminum foil and bake in a preheated 350°F. oven for 30 minutes, or until fish tests done when flaked with a fork. With a blunt knife scrape off trout skin and lift off top half of fish to a serving platter. Pull off any bones that remain. Gently turn over the trout, scrape off skin on the second side, and lift off bottom half of fish to the platter. Keep fish warm. Strain marinade. Snip enough of remaining dill to make about 6 tablespoons. In a small skillet, melt butter and sauté walnut halves until just golden. Reheat strained marinade, pour over trout, sprinkle with snipped dill, and garnish with buttered walnuts.

MAKES 2 SERVINGS.

ASPARAGUS-STUFFED TROUT FILLETS WITH MOUSSELINE SAUCE

four 6- to 8-ounce fillets of brook,
brown, or rainbow trout, skinned
twenty-four 3-inch-long asparagus
spears, cooked
salt and freshly ground pepper
⅓ cup butter, melted
juice of 1 lemon
¼ teaspoon fines herbes
Mousseline Sauce (recipe follows)
garnish: tomato and fresh parsley

Wrap each fillet around six asparagus spears. Fasten with food picks. Stand fillets upright, side by side, on a buttered shallow baking pan. Sprinkle with salt and pepper. Mix melted butter, lemon juice, and fines herbes. With a pastry brush, spread mixture over the trout and asparagus. Bake in a preheated 350°F. oven for 30 minutes, or until trout are cooked. Spoon pan juices over trout from time to time during baking.

While trout are baking, prepare Mousseline Sauce and keep warm. When trout are ready, place on a warmed serving platter lined with hot cooked saffron rice. Spoon sauce over trout and serve at once, garnished with tomato wedges and parsley sprigs.

MAKES 4 SERVINGS.

Mousseline Sauce

3 tablespoons butter
3 tablespoons flour
¼ cup dry sherry
1 cup light cream
½ cup heavy cream, whipped
Salt and freshly ground pepper
to taste

In a saucepan, melt the butter, stir in the flour, and cook over low heat until well blended. Stir in sherry and light cream. Stir over medium heat until sauce bubbles and thickens. Remove from heat. Fold in whipped cream and season with salt and pepper.

MAKES APPROXIMATELY 2 CUPS.

BAKED HERB-STUFFED TROUT

four 1-pound brook, brown, or rainbow trout, dressed
salt and freshly ground pepper
2 tablespoons minced fresh parsley, or 2 teaspoons dried parsley
2 tablespoons minced fresh tarragon, or 2 teaspoons dried tarragon
2 tablespoons minced fresh chives, or 2 teaspoons dried chives
2 tablespoons fresh thyme, or 2 teaspoons dried thyme
⅓ cup butter, melted
1 teaspoon paprika
1 ounce Cognac
juice of 1 orange
garnish: ferns and pine twigs

Score trout (slash diagonally) three times. Sprinkle trout with salt and pepper. In a small bowl, combine herbs and use the mixture to stuff the slashes in the trout. Place trout side by side in a buttered shallow baking pan. Mix remaining ingredients and spoon over trout. Bake in a preheated 350°F. oven for 20 to 25 minutes, or until trout are lightly browned. Serve garnished with ferns and pine twigs.

MAKES 4 SERVINGS.

GREEN FETTUCINI WITH TROUT CREAM SAUCE

four 12-inch trout, filleted and skinned
¼ cup butter
¼ cup flour
½ cup dry white wine
1½ cups light cream
¼ cup freshly grated Parmesan cheese
¼ cup freshly grated Romano cheese
2 tablespoons chopped fresh chives
salt and freshly ground pepper
1 pound uncooked green fettucini

Cut trout fillets into 1-inch-wide strips. In a heavy skillet, melt butter and sauté trout for 5 to 6 minutes, or until cooked. Remove trout pieces; set aside. Stir flour into pan drippings, add wine and cream. Cook, stirring, over medium heat until sauce thickens and bubbles. Stir in cheese, chives, cooked trout, and salt and pepper to taste. Meanwhile, in a large pot, bring to a boil 5 to 6 quarts water, add 1 tablespoon salt and the fettucini. Cook about 10 minutes, or until *al dente*; drain. Place fettucini on warmed serving plates and top with sauce. Serve sprinkled with additional grated Parmesan cheese.

MAKES 4 SERVINGS.

SPAGHETTI WITH TROUT MARINARA

four 12-inch trout, filleted and skinned
¼ cup olive oil
1 clove garlic, finely chopped
1 onion, chopped
½ pound fresh mushrooms, sliced
3 cups tomato sauce
½ teaspoon minced fresh oregano
½ teaspoon minced fresh basil
salt
1 pound uncooked spaghetti

Cut trout fillets into 1-inch-wide strips and set aside. In a saucepan, heat oil and sauté garlic, onion, and mushrooms for 5 minutes. Add fillet strips to skillet, as well as tomato sauce, oregano, and basil. Simmer gently for 10 minutes, stirring occasionally. Season with salt to taste. Prepare spaghetti as described above. Place on warmed serving plates and top with sauce. Serve sprinkled with additional Parmesan cheese.

MAKES 4 SERVINGS.

SOUFFLÉED STUFFED TROUT

3 pounds (3 to 6 fish) dressed spotted
sea trout (fresh or frozen)
¾ pound shelled and deveined
raw shrimps
3 egg whites
salt
freshly ground white pepper
freshly grated nutmeg
1½ cups heavy cream, chilled
3 tablespoons butter or
margarine, melted
3 tablespoons flour
¼ teaspoon paprika
¾ cup fish stock or chicken stock
¾ cup dry white wine

Thaw fish if frozen. Pat fish with paper towels to dry. Make shrimp mousseline. Cut shrimps in half if large; chill thoroughly. Drop ¼ pound of the shrimps into a blender; add 1 of the egg whites, ¼ teaspoon salt, and dash of pepper and nutmeg; blend until shrimps are pureed and a thick paste forms. Slowly pour in ⅓ cup of the cream, blending on low speed. After cream is added, turn machine to high, and blend until mixture becomes thick and light. Empty blender container and repeat process twice more in order to blend all the shrimps. (If you have a food processor, shrimp mousseline may be made all at one time: With the machine fitted with the steel blade, start machine and drop chopped shrimps in slowly; add egg whites and seasoning; slowly pour in cream.) Spread some of the shrimp mousseline in belly cavity of each fish. Place stuffed fish in a well-greased 13-by-9-by-2-inch baking pan. Brush fish with 2 tablespoons of the melted butter or margarine. Bake in a preheated 450°F. oven for 20 to 25 minutes, or until fish flakes easily.

While fish is baking, make the sauce. In a small saucepan, melt remaining 1 tablespoon butter or margarine and stir in flour, paprika, dash of pepper, and ⅛ teaspoon salt. Stir in fish stock or chicken stock and wine. Bring to a boil, stirring constantly; boil for 2 minutes. Stir in remaining ½ cup cream. To serve, spoon a small amount of sauce over souffléed trout.

MAKES 6 SERVINGS.

RUFFINO
29
31
STORMY
VERY DRY

BRAISED SWORDFISH WITH TOMATOES

2 to 2½ pounds swordfish, in one thick piece
2 teaspoons black peppercorns
1 teaspoon salt
1 pound (10 to 12) fresh plum tomatoes, or 2 cups canned peeled plum tomatoes
1 large Bermuda onion, chopped
½ cup chopped celery leaves
6 anchovy fillets, minced
2 tablespoons capers, drained
½ cup dry white wine

With a rolling pin, crush the peppercorns; mix with the salt and spread out on a sheet of waxed paper. Press swordfish onto the salt and peppercorns, first one side, then the other, pressing firmly enough to make seasoning adhere to fish. If you are using fresh tomatoes, blanch, peel, and chop them, discarding as many seeds as possible. Oil a casserole large enough to hold the fish snugly. Put tomatoes, onion, and celery leaves into the bottom of the casserole, lay swordfish on top, and scatter anchovy pieces and 1 tablespoon capers over all. Pour in the wine. Bake, covered, in a preheated 400°F. oven for 20 minutes. Open casserole and spoon some of the vegetables and wine over fish. Cover again and continue to bake for 20 to 30 minutes longer, or until fish flakes easily when tested with a fork. Carefully transfer fish to a heatproof platter and keep warm. Puree the braising mixture, reheat it, and arrange around the fish. Garnish with remaining capers.

MAKES 8 SERVINGS.

STURGEON FILLET MARK HOPKINS

four 7-ounce center-cut fillets of sturgeon, or one 2-pound fillet of sturgeon
1/2 cup flour
3/4 cup (1 1/2 sticks) butter
1 1/4 cups dry vermouth
1 teaspoon minced shallot
1/2 clove garlic, minced
1/4 cup heavy cream
2 teaspoons beluga caviar or salmon (red) caviar
garnish: parsley sprigs, cherry tomatoes, small whole potatoes, papaya flowers

Dredge sturgeon fillets in flour and shake off excess. In a large skillet, melt the butter and sauté fish until just cooked. Transfer to a warmed plate and keep warm. Deglaze skillet with vermouth. Add shallot and garlic, and simmer until reduced to half. Add cream, and simmer for 5 minutes longer. Pour sauce over sturgeon and sprinkle with caviar. Garnish with parsley, peeled cherry tomatoes, steamed potatoes, and papaya flowers.

MAKES 4 SERVINGS.

HERBED SHAD ROE EN PAPILLOTE

1 pair shad roe
olive oil
salt
1 to 1½ teaspoons snipped fresh chives
1 to 1½ teaspoons snipped fresh dill
1 to 1½ teaspoons minced shallots
6 large fresh mushrooms, sliced
butter shavings
1 tablespoon fresh lemon juice
1 tablespoon Amontillado sherry

Carefully lay roe on oiled parchment paper (see general instructions, p. 97). Season with salt and sprinkle with fresh herbs. Place mushroom slices in overlapping leaves across top of roe. Dot with butter shavings. Sprinkle with lemon juice and sherry. Carefully bring paper up and around; fold and crimp open edges to seal. Bake in a preheated 500°F. oven for 5 minutes; reduce heat to 375°F. and bake for an additional 10 to 20 minutes, depending upon size of roe.

Great accompaniments: Fresh asparagus and a glass of chilled Amontillado sherry.

MAKES 1 SERVING.

POACHED RAY WITH BROWN BUTTER

1 ray, dressed
salt
white vinegar
3 sprigs fresh chervil
3 sprigs fresh tarragon
freshly ground pepper to taste
chopped fresh parsley
chopped fresh chervil
chopped fresh tarragon

Wash ray under running water. Scrub with a brush to remove the slimy coating. Remove wings and cut them into 10-ounce portions. Cover with water; add salt and ½ cup vinegar for each quart of water. Add chervil and tarragon. Bring water slowly to a boil and skim. Reduce heat and simmer for 15 minutes.

Pour off cooking water and carefully remove ray portions. Remove skin from both sides of pieces and arrange fish on a serving platter. While ray is hot, season with salt and freshly ground pepper. Sprinkle each portion with a pinch each of chopped parsley, chervil, and tarragon. Heat butter until brown. Pour over the fish, followed by a splash of vinegar warmed in the same pan. Serve with grated carrots, string beans, and baby ears of corn.

EACH 10-OUNCE PORTION MAKES 1 SERVING.

PICCATA OF MAKO SHARK

four 3-ounce slices mako shark, cut
very thin
salt and freshly ground pepper
flour for dredging
¼ pound (1 stick) butter
2 teaspoons capers, drained
1 lemon, peeled and sectioned
garnish: 2 teaspoons chopped fresh
parsley

Season shark slices with salt and pepper; dredge with flour and shake off excess. In a skillet, melt half the butter and heat until butter foams. Put mako slices in the pan and brown for 1 minute on each side. Remove slices to a platter and keep warm. Wipe skillet clean. Put in remaining butter and heat. When butter foams, add capers and lemon sections. Sauté for 2 minutes, remove lemon slices, then pour at once over mako. Sprinkle with chopped parsley and serve.

MAKES 2 SERVINGS.

MOET

WALLEYE QUENELLES WITH CUCUMBER SAUCE

1½ pounds walleye fillets, skinned
2 whole eggs
2 egg whites
1½ cups heavy cream
1 teaspoon salt
¼ teaspoon grated mace
2 cups chicken broth
2 cups dry white wine

Cut fillets into pieces. Place fish, whole eggs, and egg whites in a blender or food processor and whirl until smooth. Gradually add cream, salt, and mace while machine is blending. Pour into a bowl, cover, and chill for several hours.

In a large skillet, combine chicken broth and wine and bring to a simmer. Shape rounded tablespoons of the fish mixture and carefully place them in the simmering liquid. Cook for 10 minutes, or until dumplings are firm. Remove from liquid with a slotted spoon, arrange on a serving platter, and keep warm; reserve poaching liquid for sauce. Make Cucumber Sauce (recipe follows). Spoon sauce over the dumplings and garnish with cucumber slices.

MAKES 6 SERVINGS.

Cucumber Sauce

¼ cup butter
1 large cucumber, peeled, seeded, and diced
¼ cup flour
1 cup reserved poaching liquid
1 cup heavy cream, at room temperature
2 egg yolks
2 tablespoons chopped fresh dill, or 2 teaspoons dried dill
salt and freshly ground white pepper to taste

In a saucepan, melt butter and sauté cucumber for 3 or 4 minutes. Blend in flour. Gradually pour in 1 cup poaching liquid, stirring constantly. In a bowl, whisk the cream and egg yolks until smooth, then stir into saucepan. Add the dill. Continue stirring over medium heat until sauce thickens, but do not boil. Season with salt and pepper.

MAKES 2½ CUPS.

WALLEYE BAKED WITH RATATOUILLE

two 2-pound walleye, dressed
salt and freshly ground pepper
¼ cup olive oil
2 cloves garlic, finely chopped
1 onion, chopped
1 eggplant, cut into 1-inch cubes
2 zucchini, diced
¼ pound fresh mushrooms, sliced
4 large ripe tomatoes, diced
1 teaspoon *herbes de Provence*

Sprinkle walleye with salt and pepper and place in a shallow baking pan; set aside. In a large saucepan, heat oil and sauté garlic and onion for 5 minutes. Add remaining ingredients and stir. Simmer, covered, for 10 minutes. Season to taste with salt and pepper. Pour mixture over fish. Cover with aluminum foil and bake in a preheated 350°F. oven for 30 to 35 minutes, or until fish are cooked. Serve walleye with ratatouille spooned over them.

MAKES 4 SERVINGS.

TILEFISH FILLETS WITH ORANGE SAUCE

2 pounds tilefish fillets
½ cup frozen orange juice concentrate, thawed
1 teaspoon salt
dash of freshly ground pepper
1½ cups cornflake crumbs
¼ cup butter or margarine, melted
Orange Sauce (recipe follows)

Cut fillets into serving-size portions. Combine orange juice concentrate, salt, and pepper. Dip fish into orange juice and roll in cornflake crumbs. Place fish in a single layer in a well-greased baking pan. Pour melted butter or margarine over fish. Bake in an extremely hot preheated 500°F. oven for 8 to 10 minutes, or until fillets are browned and fish separates easily when tested with a fork. While fish is baking, make Orange Sauce and keep warm. Serve with sauce.

MAKES 6 SERVINGS.

Orange Sauce

2 tablespoons white wine vinegar
1½ tablespoons sugar
½ cup chicken broth
¼ cup frozen orange juice concentrate, thawed
¼ cup water
1 tablespoon grated orange rind
¼ cup dry white wine
1 tablespoon cornstarch

In a 1-quart saucepan, combine vinegar and sugar. Boil until syrup begins to caramelize and turns brown. Remove pan from heat and pour in chicken broth. Simmer, stirring constantly, for 1 minute longer, or until caramel is dissolved. Add orange juice concentrate, water, and orange rind. In a cup, combine wine and cornstarch; add to orange mixture and cook, stirring constantly, until thick.

MAKES ABOUT 1 CUP.

ABALONE WITH GRAPE SAUCE

12 abalone steaks
Grape Sauce (recipe follows)
½ cup sugar
1½ cups hot water
½ pound green seedless grapes
2 oranges
1 cup milk
½ cup flour
3 eggs, beaten
¼ pound salted butter
salt and freshly ground pepper
to taste

Make Grape Sauce and keep warm. Pound abalone steaks thin and pat dry. Dissolve sugar in hot water to make a sugar syrup. In a saucepan, gently poach grapes in sugar syrup for 5 minutes, or until tender; set aside. Cut each orange into six slices; discard ends and remove any seeds; set aside. Moisten abalone in milk, sprinkle with flour, then dip into beaten eggs. In a large, flat skillet, melt butter and sauté abalone over high heat to a golden-yellow color, about 30 seconds on each side. Season with salt and pepper. Arrange steaks, alternating with orange slices, overlapping in a row on a warmed serving platter. Sprinkle poached grapes over and cover with sauce.

MAKES 12 SERVINGS.

Grape Sauce

1 teaspoon chopped shallots
1 cup dry red wine
1 cup grape juice extracted from
1 to 2 pounds fresh grapes
1 teaspoon Cognac
1 tablespoon cream

In a saucepan, combine shallots, wine, and grape juice. Over low heat reduce liquid to half. Stir in Cognac and cream; heat sauce thoroughly, then serve.

MAKES ABOUT 1 CUP.

CALAMARI SALAD WITH CHAMPAGNE DRESSING

2 pounds baby squid, dressed
white wine
water
2 cups baby peas, cooked
1 cup thinly sliced celery
2 ripe tomatoes, chopped
1 red onion, thinly sliced
2 cups cooked saffron rice
Champagne Dressing (recipe follows)
garnish: lettuce cups

Cut squid into crosswise slices and leave tentacles whole. Poach 4 to 5 minutes in equal parts white wine and water. In a large serving bowl, mix squid with peas, celery, tomatoes, onion, and rice. Make Champagne Dressing, pour over salad, and toss to coat all particles. Chill for several hours to blend flavors. Toss again before serving in lettuce cups with slices of crusty bread.

MAKES 6 SERVINGS.

Champagne Dressing

½ cup olive oil
1 clove garlic, crushed
¼ cup red wine vinegar
½ cup champagne
½ teaspoon fines herbes
salt and freshly ground pepper to taste

In a jar with a tight-fitting lid, combine dressing ingredients, except salt and pepper, and shake until thick and well blended. Season with salt and pepper.

MAKES ABOUT 1¼ CUPS.

CLAMS CASINO

6 cherrystone clams
juice of 1/4 lemon
1/4 pound (1 stick) butter, softened
1 tablespoon anchovy paste
1/2 teaspoon minced garlic
1 tablespoon diced pimiento
1 tablespoon minced onion
1 tablespoon minced green pepper
four 1 1/2-inch-long slices
medium-cut bacon

Shuck clams and remove meats from shell; reserve four shells. Coarsely chop the meats and spoon back evenly into the four shells. Sprinkle evenly with lemon juice. In a small bowl, combine butter, anchovy paste, garlic, pimiento, onion, and green pepper; mix thoroughly. Fill clam shells with equal amounts of the mixture, and top each shell with a strip of bacon.

Set filled clam shells in a pie pan half-filled with rock salt. Bake in a preheated 450°F. oven for about 6 minutes, or until bacon is just crisp and the ingredients have married.

This appetizer recipe, which can be safely multiplied, is for one serving, based on six clam meats for each serving of four clams on the half shell. The additional bits of meat "plump" the final product and enhance both texture and flavor.

MAKES 1 SERVING.

CLAM FRITTERS

12 chowder-size hard-shell clams,
or two 8-ounce cans
minced clams
½ cup pancake mix
⅓ cup flour
1 teaspoon seafood seasoning
½ teaspoon dried parsley flakes
salt and freshly ground pepper
to taste
1 egg
½ cup reserved clam juice
few drops liquid hot pepper sauce
fat or oil for frying

Shuck clams, reserving liquor, and chop; or drain canned clams, reserving broth. In a large bowl, combine pancake mix, flour, seafood seasoning, parsley flakes, and salt and pepper; mix well. In a small bowl, beat egg and reserved clam juice and liquid hot pepper sauce. Stir egg mixture into flour mixture. Stir in clams.

Heat a griddle or skillet to 350°F., adding just enough fat or oil to prevent sticking. Drop batter by tablespoonfuls onto pan and cook pancakes for 2 to 3 minutes, or until browned. Turn carefully and brown the other side.

MAKES ABOUT EIGHT 3½-INCH FRITTERS.

CLAM POFFERTJES

1 cup finely minced clams
1⅓ cups sifted flour
2 teaspoons baking powder
¾ teaspoon salt
½ teaspoon garlic powder
½ teaspoon cayenne pepper
2 egg yolks
½ cup milk
3 tablespoons minced onion
2 tablespoons lemon juice
2 egg whites, stiffly beaten

In a small bowl, combine flour, baking powder, salt, garlic powder, and cayenne pepper. In a large bowl, beat egg yolks and milk together. Gradually add the dry ingredients to the eggs and milk and mix thoroughly. Stir in onion, clams, and lemon juice. Fold egg whites into clam batter.

Heat *poffertjes* pan and grease depressions with unsalted butter. Spoon batter by tablespoonfuls into depressions and cook for 30 seconds, turn with fork and cook on other side for 30 seconds, or until lightly browned. Slide *poffertjes* onto a warmed platter and serve with grated cheese.

MAKES 60 SERVINGS FOR 6 TO 8 PEOPLE.

NOTE: *Minced shrimp, crab meat, or lobster may be substituted for clams.*

OLD-LINE OYSTER PIE

1 pint shucked oysters, with liquor
pastry for double-crust 9-inch pie
2 cups thinly sliced potatoes, slightly undercooked and well drained
4 eggs, hard-cooked, shelled, and sliced
¼ cup butter or margarine
celery salt to taste
lemon-and-pepper seasoning to taste
Oyster Sauce (recipe follows)

Place bottom layer of pastry in pie pan. Put in potatoes. Drain oysters by removing them from container with a slotted spoon, then arrange them over potatoes; reserve oyster liquor for sauce. Place egg slices over oysters. Dot butter or margarine over top and sprinkle with celery salt and lemon-and-pepper seasoning. Place remaining layer of pastry on top of pie. Cut slits in top to allow steam to escape. Bake in a preheated 400°F. oven for 10 minutes; reduce heat to 375°F. and bake for about 30 minutes longer, or until crust is lightly browned. Let stand for a few minutes before serving. While pie is baking, make Oyster Sauce and keep warm. Serve with sauce.

MAKES 6 SERVINGS.

Oyster Sauce

2 tablespoons butter or margarine
2 tablespoons flour
1 cup milk
oyster liquor plus water to equal ½ cup
salt and freshly ground pepper to taste

In a medium saucepan, melt butter or margarine; mix in flour. Slowly add milk, then oyster liquor, stirring constantly to keep mixture smooth and free from lumps. Cook, stirring, over medium heat until mixture comes to a boil and thickens. Season with salt and pepper.

MAKES ABOUT 1½ CUPS.

FISHERMAN'S OYSTER STEW

32 oysters, shucked, without liquor
¾ cup light cream
¾ cup clam juice
½ teaspoon celery salt
5 drops Tabasco
6 tablespoons butter
garnish: paprika

In a saucepan, combine cream, clam juice, celery salt, and Tabasco. Over low heat, bring the cream mixture to a simmer; do not let it boil at any time. Bring water to boil in bottom part of double boiler, and reduce to simmer, making sure water clears top part by ½ inch. In top part, melt butter and add oysters, stirring with a wooden spoon or paddle to let them heat evenly until the edges curl. Pour the hot cream mixture into the oysters. Let the stew reach a simmer; do not let it boil.

Ladle into four deep bowls and sprinkle with paprika. Serve at once.

MAKES 4 SERVINGS.

NOTE: *For a less creamy stew, use half-and-half instead of light cream. Use more celery salt and Tabasco to taste if you prefer. If cream is used, the stew is buttery enough without additional butter; if half-and-half is used, you may wish to drop a pat of butter (½ tablespoon) into each bowl at serving time. If you are using unsalted butter, you may want to add a pinch of salt to the stew.*

Boordy

OYSTERS CHANCERY

1 pint shucked Maryland oysters (standards or selects), without liquor
1 tablespoon chicken-seasoned stock base, or 1 chicken bouillon cube
2 cups boiling water
6 tablespoons butter or margarine
3 tablespoons flour
1 tablespoon arrowroot dissolved in 2 tablespoons water (optional)
½ cup sliced fresh mushrooms
¼ cup coarsely chopped Smithfield ham
1 heaping tablespoon chopped fresh chives or green onion
1 tablespoon sherry
1 tablespoon minced onion
½ teaspoon lemon-and-pepper seasoning
½ medium clove garlic, crushed
8 patty shells, prepared according to package directions
garnish: fresh parsley and paprika

Dissolve chicken stock base or bouillon cube in boiling water. In a 2-quart saucepan, melt 4 tablespoons of the butter or margarine and stir in flour, blending until hot and bubbly. Slowly add chicken broth, stirring constantly to keep smooth and free from lumps. Cook over medium heat until mixture comes to a boil and thickens, 10 or 15 minutes. (If additional thickening is desired, add arrowroot-water solution.) Reduce heat, add mushrooms, ham, chives or green onion, sherry, onion, seasoning, and garlic. Simmer for 2 or 3 minutes, or until blended. Set aside, stirring occasionally until used.

In a 2-quart saucepan, simmer oysters until edges just begin to curl. Drain and rinse to free oysters from cooking residue and excess liquid; add oysters to sauce. In a small saucepan, melt remaining 2 tablespoons butter or margarine; add to sauce. Fill patty shells with oyster mixture and sprinkle with chopped parsley and paprika. Place on a baking sheet and broil, 4 inches from source of heat, for 1 or 2 minutes, or until hot and bubbly. Serve immediately.

MAKES 8 SERVINGS AS A FIRST COURSE OR 4 SERVINGS AS AN ENTRÉE.

HANGTOWN FRY

1 pint shucked oysters (standards or selects), without liquor
3 slices bacon, cut in 1-inch-long pieces
1/2 cup dry bread or cracker crumbs
1/3 cup flour
1/4 cup milk
1/4 cup butter or margarine, melted, or 1/4 cup oil
8 eggs, separated
1/4 cup water
1/2 teaspoon salt
dash of freshly ground pepper
garnish: 2 teaspoons minced fresh parsley, lemon

In a 10-inch skillet, fry bacon until crisp. Drain on absorbent paper, but reserve drippings in skillet. Set aside six pieces of bacon for garnish. In a bowl or on a plate, combine bread or cracker crumbs and flour. Dip oysters into milk, then into crumb mixture. Fry oysters in bacon drippings plus half the liquid fat for 2 to 3 minutes on each side, or until lightly browned. Set aside six oysters for garnish. Sprinkle bacon pieces over oysters in skillet.

In a bowl, combine egg yolks, water, remaining liquid fat, salt, and pepper; beat briskly and set aside. In a 2-quart bowl, beat egg whites until stiff peaks form. Fold yolk mixture carefully into whites. Heat skillet containing oysters and bacon, and pour egg mixture over them. Cook omelet until bottom browns lightly. Arrange reserved oysters and bacon pieces on top of omelet as garnish. Transfer skillet to a preheated 350°F. oven and bake for 15 to 20 minutes, or until top is light golden brown. Garnish with minced parsley and lemon wedges. Serve at once.

MAKES 6 SERVINGS.

COLD STUFFED MUSSELS

36 mussels
½ cup olive oil
3 red onions, minced
¼ cup pine nuts, chopped
¼ cup dried currants, chopped
1 cup uncooked long-grain rice
¼ teaspoon ground cinnamon
¼ teaspoon ground allspice
2 tablespoons chopped fresh parsley
salt to taste
3⅓ cups boiling water
1 ounce fino sherry

With a stiff brush, vigorously scrub mussels under cold running water. With a small sharp knife, pry open each mussel, taking care not to break hinge at narrow end of shells. Scrape off tufty beard; remove black part of meat. Place opened mussels in a deep pan of cold water as you go. Rinse carefully in several changes of water, leaving them in final change of clear water until ready to use.

In a skillet with a tight-fitting lid, heat oil and sauté onions until lightly browned and translucent. Stir in pine nuts and dried currants; cook for a few minutes. Stir in rice, cover, and cook for about 5 minutes more. Add cinnamon, allspice, parsley, salt, and 1⅓ cups boiling water. Cover tightly and cook over low heat until water is absorbed and rice is tender, about 20 minutes. Leave covered the entire time; slip a slow-heating pad between skillet and heat if heat cannot be adjusted low enough. Turn off heat and let rice rest for 5 minutes without removing cover. Add sherry and toss.

Drain cleaned mussels. Fill empty half of shell with rice mixture. Close shell, hold firmly together, and tie with heavy thread or light string. Place mussels in tightly packed layers in a large Dutch oven. Pour in 2 cups boiling water; carefully weight mussels with a heavy heatproof plate or appropriate alternative. Cover tightly; steam over low heat for about 20 minutes. Allow to cool. Carefully remove mussels with slotted spoon and cut string or thread. Chill in refrigerator until ready to serve.

MAKES 6 SERVINGS.

NOTE: *Mussels may be rinsed under running water several times the night before without opening them. After rinsing, put them in a bowl of clear water with a fistful of flour or cornmeal. The mussels will clean themselves out by gorging on the flour. When ready to proceed, rinse mussels thoroughly, open, and continue as directed.*

MUSSEL RISOTTO

5 pounds mussels
2 large cloves garlic
10 sprigs fresh parsley
½ cup olive oil
½ pound onions, chopped
8 fresh basil leaves, or
  1 teaspoon dried basil
½ teaspoon whole saffron or
  ground turmeric
2 cups white wine
approximately 2 cups fish stock
2 red bell peppers, chopped
2 cups uncooked brown rice
1 teaspoon salt

With a stiff brush, scrub mussels vigorously under cold running water and remove beards. Peel garlic, leave whole, and insert a wooden food pick in each clove. Remove leafy tops of parsley for later, and chop stems into small pieces. In a deep kettle large enough to hold the mussels, heat 5 tablespoons of the oil and sauté onions and garlic until onions are translucent. Lift out and discard garlic. Add parsley stems, basil, saffron or turmeric, and wine. Bring to a simmer, then add scrubbed mussels. Cover the kettle and steam mussels over moderate heat. Use two skimmers to lift mussels in the bottom to the top so that all steam evenly. Steam only until mussels are opened. Remove kettle from heat. When cool enough to handle, remove mussels from shells. Discard all shells and any mussels that have not opened. Pour juices in the kettle through a sieve lined with a dampened cloth, and measure. Add enough fish stock to make 5 cups liquid; set aside.

In a large saucepan, heat remaining 3 tablespoons oil and sauté peppers until tender. With a slotted spoon, transfer peppers to a plate. Add rice to oil in saucepan and sauté over moderate heat until kernels begin to turn white. Pour in the reserved 5 cups liquid and the salt (adjust salt if fish stock was already salted). Bring to a boil, reduce to a simmer, cover, and cook for 15 to 20 minutes, or until rice is nearly tender. Reserve several mussels for garnish. Stir in sautéed peppers and remainder of shelled mussels, and leave over heat only long enough to reheat shellfish. Spoon out onto a deep, round serving platter. Chop reserved leafy parsley tops and sprinkle over risotto. Serve with fresh asparagus and an orange and red-onion salad.

MAKES 8 TO 10 SERVINGS.

SCALLOPS AND MUSSELS IN MUSTARD VINAIGRETTE ON ASPARAGUS

60 bay scallops
60 cooked mussels, shucked
1/4 cup lemon juice
Boston lettuce
36 to 48 stalks fresh asparagus,
 slightly undercooked
 and well drained
garnish: fresh parsley, red bell pepper

Marinate scallop meats in lemon juice for 1 hour. Drain scallops and mix with mussels. Make Dijon Mustard Vinaigrette (recipe follows). Gently toss shellfish with dressing. On six large individual salad plates, arrange a bed of lettuce leaves and lay equal portions of asparagus on top. Arrange shellfish with dressing across the asparagus. Sprinkle with chopped parsley and pepper slices.

MAKES 6 SERVINGS.

Dijon Mustard Vinaigrette

1 egg yolk
1 egg, hard-cooked, chopped
1/4 cup prepared Dijon mustard
1 tablespoon minced onion
2 teaspoons minced shallot
1 clove garlic, minced
2 teaspoons minced fresh parsley
 (or more according to taste)
2 teaspoons minced fresh oregano
1 teaspoon minced fresh basil
1/2 teaspoon salt
several grinds of black pepper
pinch of sugar
1 cup olive oil
3 tablespoons white wine
3 tablespoons white vinegar

In a deep, narrow bowl, combine first twelve ingredients. Slowly beat in the oil, adding it alternately with mixed wine and vinegar. Combine each portion well before adding the next.

MAKES ABOUT 2 CUPS.

SCALLOPS WITH LEMON DRESSING

24 scallops, with roe if possible
2 small leeks, white parts only, finely shredded
1 carrot, finely shredded
1 quart fish stock
16 lettuce leaves
Lemon Dressing (recipe follows)
garnish: leeks, carrot strips

Put leeks and carrots in a small saucepan, cover with water, and simmer for 10 minutes; drain. Meanwhile, in a large saucepan, bring fish stock to a boil, then set scallops in a colander or strainer and poach in the stock for about 5 minutes or until stock reaches the boiling point again. Remove scallops and set aside. Keep warm and make Lemon Dressing.

Place four lettuce leaves on each of four individual salad plates, arranging scallops on center. Sprinkle leeks and carrots on top of scallops. Spoon warm dressing over all.

MAKES 4 SERVINGS.

Lemon Dressing

juice of 2 lemons
1 tablespoon olive oil
pinch of dry mustard
salt and freshly ground pepper to taste

In a bowl, mix the lemon juice, olive oil, mustard, and salt and pepper. Keep dressing warm in the top part of a double boiler until ready to serve.

MAKES 1/3 CUP OR 4 SERVINGS.

NOTE: *The red-leaf lettuce from California adds a nice touch.*

SCALLOP SALAD DOLPHIN STRIKER

1½ pounds whole bay scallops or halved sea scallops
2 cups white wine
2 cups water
2 stems fresh parsley
½ teaspoon minced fresh tarragon
½ cup coarsely chopped onion
1 bay leaf
½ pound small whole fresh mushrooms
¼ cup minced celery
2 tablespoons capers, drained
¼ cup minced onion
salt and pepper to taste
approximately ½ cup mayonnaise
garnish: romaine lettuce, capers, red pepper

In a large saucepan, combine wine and water. Add scallops, parsley stems, tarragon, coarsely chopped onion, and bay leaf. Bring to a boil, then poach over low heat for 2½ minutes. Add mushrooms and continue poaching for another 2½ minutes. Let pan cool and place in refrigerator to chill.

When chilled, drain, removing parsley stems and coarsely chopped onion. Add celery, capers, and minced onion. Season with salt and pepper. Spoon on enough mayonnaise to bind the ingredients, and toss salad lightly. Serve on a bed of romaine lettuce garnished with capers and/or diced red pepper.

MAKES 4 OR 5 SERVINGS AS A FIRST COURSE.

SCALLOP AND SHRIMP MARUCCA

1¼ pounds scallops
8 large fresh shrimps, butterflied
Garlic Butter (recipe follows)
4 medium fresh mushrooms, sliced
4 tablespoons sherry
garnish: paprika

Make Garlic Butter and keep warm. Place one shrimp at each end of four individual casserole dishes so that tail fin protrudes from the dish (as shown). Scatter mushroom slices in bottoms of casseroles. Pack scallops with 2 tablespoons Garlic Butter per dish. Sprinkle with sherry and dust lightly with paprika. Bake in a preheated 400°F. oven for 15 minutes.

MAKES 4 SERVINGS.

Garlic Butter

¼ pound (1 stick) butter
1 tablespoon minced garlic

In a saucepan, melt butter, add garlic, and simmer until garlic turns blond. Strain.

MAKES ½ CUP.

SCALLOPS AND SHRIMPS À LA CHINOISE

1 pound sea scallops
1 pound shelled and deveined raw shrimps, weighed after shelling
6 dried black mushrooms
12 water chestnuts
6 whole green onions, cut into 1½-inch slivers
1 teaspoon grated fresh gingerroot
1 teaspoon honey
2 teaspoons soy sauce
¼ cup chicken stock
3 tablespoons oil
2 large green peppers, cut into 1½-inch-wide slivers
garnish: watercress

Rinse scallops, pat dry, and cut each into two or three round slices. Rinse shrimps, pat dry, and split lengthwise. Soak mushrooms 30 minutes in warm water to cover. Cut water chestnuts into slices about as thick as scallop slices. Mix green and white parts of green onion slivers together and set aside half for garnish. In a bowl, mix gingerroot, honey, soy sauce, and chicken stock; set aside. Lift mushrooms from soaking liquid; pour liquid through a cloth-lined sieve and reserve. Discard mushroom stems (they are tough), and slice the caps.

In a wok, heat the oil to very hot. Put in green pepper slivers and half of green onion slivers, and stir-fry for 1 minute. Add water chestnuts and mushrooms, and stir-fry for another minute. Push vegetables to the side and add scallops and shrimps. Stir-fry for 2 minutes, then mix vegetables and seafood together. Add the liquid mixture as well as the reserved mushroom soaking liquid; cook, stirring, until seafood pieces are just tender (vegetables should still be crunchy). Serve on warmed plates, with rice; garnish each serving with some of the reserved slivered green onions and a sprinkle of watercress leaves.

MAKES 8 SERVINGS.

NOTE: *If you don't have a wok, this can be cooked in a deep skillet; in that case you may need a little additional oil.*

SHRIMP AND MUSHROOM QUICHE

1 pound (61 to 70) small shrimps, cooked, shelled, and deveined
pastry for single-crust 9-inch pie
1 cup sliced fresh mushrooms
2 tablespoons freshly grated Gruyère cheese
4 whole eggs, separated
2 egg yolks
1 teaspoon salt
½ teaspoon freshly ground pepper
3 drops Tabasco
1 cup light cream
garnish: paprika

Fit pastry into quiche pan; prick entire bottom of pastry with a fork. Refrigerate pastry for 1 hour. Brown pastry lightly in a preheated 350°F. oven for 5 to 7 minutes. Cover pastry bottom with mushrooms. Arrange shrimps over mushrooms. Sprinkle with grated cheese. In a small bowl, beat the 6 egg yolks; add salt, pepper, and Tabasco. Whisk in cream until well blended. In a bowl, beat the 4 egg whites until very thick (not stiff) and fold into the custard mixture. Pour mixture into pastry shell. Lightly sprinkle with paprika. Bake in 375°F. oven for 35 to 45 minutes, or until pastry is golden brown and custard has set.

MAKES 6 SERVINGS.

NOTE: *The quiche can be baked in a frozen piecrust; puncture four or five holes in the bottom of the pastry before browning it.*

Piecrust can be made from traditional pâte brisée *(2 cups flour, ½ teaspoon salt, ¼ pound butter, ½ cup cold water), which holds up well. For a very flaky crust, use an oil pastry (2 cups flour, ½ teaspoon salt, ½ cup oil, ¼ cup milk).*

ROCK SHRIMP NEWBURG

The rock shrimp has a very hard shell, but a peeling machine was invented in 1970 that made mass production possible. It can also be cut down the middle on the ventral side, as one would split a lobster. If you buy them peeled and deveined, the cooking time in boiling water is 20 seconds; if in the shell, 2 minutes. In either form, rinse under cold water immediately to stop the cooking action. The rock shrimp is more lobsterlike in texture and flavor than our common peneid shrimps.

1 pound cooked rock shrimp meat
¼ cup butter or margarine
2 tablespoons flour
¾ teaspoon salt
¼ teaspoon paprika
dash of cayenne pepper
2 cups light cream
2 egg yolks, beaten
1½ to 2 tablespoons sherry
6 baked patty shells

In a heavy saucepan, melt butter or margarine and blend in flour, salt, paprika, and cayenne pepper. Add cream gradually and cook over medium heat, stirring constantly, until sauce is thick and smooth. Stir a little of the hot sauce into egg yolks to equalize temperature; add egg yolks to remaining sauce, stirring constantly. Add rock shrimp meat; heat. Remove from heat and slowly stir in sherry. Serve immediately in patty shells.

MAKES 6 SERVINGS AS A FIRST COURSE.

SWEET AND SOUR ROCK SHRIMP TAILS

1 pound cooked, peeled, and deveined
rock shrimps
¼ cup margarine or oil
1 medium onion, thinly sliced
1 small green pepper, cut into
1-inch squares
two 8¼-ounce cans pineapple
chunks in heavy syrup
½ cup white vinegar
¼ cup sugar
2 tablespoons cornstarch
1 tablespoon soy sauce
½ teaspoon dry mustard
¼ teaspoon salt
⅔ cup halved cherry tomatoes
or thin tomato wedges
½ cup slivered almonds, toasted
3 cups cooked rice, hot

Cut large shrimps in half. In a skillet, heat margarine or oil and sauté onion and green pepper until tender but not brown. Drain pineapple chunks and reserve syrup. In a jar, combine pineapple syrup, vinegar, sugar, cornstarch, soy sauce, dry mustard, and salt; shake together until well blended; add to vegetables in skillet. Cook, stirring constantly, until thick and clear. Gently stir in pineapple chunks, cherry tomatoes or tomato wedges, and shrimps, and heat thoroughly. Stir almonds into cooked rice. Serve sweet and sour mixture over almond rice.

MAKES 6 SERVINGS.

JAPANESE PRICKLY SHRIMPS

1½ pounds raw shrimps, shelled and deveined
2 teaspoons dry sherry
1 tablespoon minced fresh gingerroot
2 tablespoons minced scallions
1 tablespoon Japanese soy sauce
½ clove garlic, chopped
1 egg white
uncooked vermicelli or Japanese sōmen noodles
fat or oil for deep frying
garnish: scallions and pine twigs

Finely chop shrimps or chop in a food processor. Place shrimps in a medium bowl and stir in sherry, gingerroot, scallions, soy sauce, garlic, and egg white. With moist hands, shape the mixture into balls. Break noodles into 1½-inch lengths. Roll balls in noodles, pressing noodles into balls for a prickly effect. In a heavy skillet, heat fat or oil to 360°F. Drop the balls into the fat and fry for 5 or 6 minutes, or until noodles are lightly browned and shrimp mixture turns pink. Serve hot accompanied with soy sauce mixed with sliced scallions. Garnish with sliced scallions and pine twigs.

MAKES ABOUT 18 BALLS.

UKOY

½ pound (40 to 50) fresh shrimps, shelled
Garlic-Vinegar Sauce (recipe follows)
2 eggs
¼ cup milk
½ cup flour
2 cups fresh bean sprouts
oil for deep frying

Make Garlic-Vinegar Sauce and let stand. In a saucepan, bring water to boil and blanch shrimps for 45 seconds. In a bowl, beat eggs and milk, then add flour, stirring, but not too well, to make a lumpy batter. Add the bean sprouts and mix with a fork. Add the shrimps and continue to mix until the ingredients are coated with batter. In a deep fryer, heat oil to 375°F. Using a fork and tablespoon, form generous spoonfuls of the *ukoy* mixture, putting individual "nests" into the bubbling oil. Cook for 30 seconds on each side, or until just browned. Serve with sauce.

MAKES 4 SERVINGS.

Garlic-Vinegar Sauce

4 cloves garlic, pressed
¾ cup white vinegar
¼ cup water
¼ teaspoon freshly ground black pepper
¼ teaspoon salt

Combine all ingredients and allow to stand for at least 1 hour.

MAKES ABOUT 1 CUP.

CRAB MEAT PARFAIT

1 pound fresh crab meat, cooked
1 cup sour cream
½ cup mayonnaise
1½ cups diced cucumber
6 tablespoons chopped fresh chives
juice of 1 lemon
salt to taste
garnish: 4 ounces salmon (red) caviar,
6 round slices lemon

In a bowl, thoroughly mix sour cream and mayonnaise. Toss crab meat with the dressing to coat thoroughly; keep chilled. In a smaller bowl, mix cucumber and chives. Sprinkle with lemon juice and salt and toss to blend.

With a soup spoon, make a layer of cucumber mixture in the bottom of each of six parfait glasses. Next make a wider layer of crab meat on top of the cucumber in each glass. Then another layer of cucumber, topped with another layer of crab meat. Finish with a splash of the sour cream dressing and decorate with berries of salmon caviar and lemon rounds.

MAKES SIX 6-OUNCE SERVINGS AS A FIRST COURSE.

SAN FRANCISCO CRAB SOUP

2 cups cooked Dungeness crab meat
(2 crabs, about 1½ pounds each)
¼ cup butter
1 medium onion, chopped
1 green pepper, chopped
1 leek, white part only, chopped
2 quarts fish stock
½ cup uncooked rice
3 ripe tomatoes, peeled, seeded, and diced
½ pound fresh okra, cut into crosswise slices
1 teaspoon Worcestershire sauce
salt and freshly ground pepper to taste
garnish: fresh parsley

In a 3-quart saucepan, melt the butter and simmer the vegetables until tender. Add stock and rice, bring to a boil, and simmer, covered, for 20 minutes. Add tomatoes, okra, and Worcestershire sauce to stock with crab meat. Bring again to a boil, then simmer for 20 minutes. Season with salt and pepper. Sprinkle with chopped parsley.

MAKES 6 TO 8 SERVINGS.

MARYLAND CRAB CAKES

1 pound fresh backfin crab meat
½ cup bread crumbs
1 egg, beaten
5 tablespoons mayonnaise
1 tablespoon minced fresh parsley
2 teaspoons Worcestershire sauce
1 teaspoon prepared mustard
1 teaspoon salt
¼ teaspoon freshly ground white pepper
fat or oil for deep frying, or butter for sautéeing

Remove cartilage from crab meat. In a bowl, mix bread crumbs, egg, mayonnaise, parsley, Worcestershire sauce, mustard, salt, and white pepper together well. Pour mixture over crab meat and fold in lightly but thoroughly. Form into six cakes. Deep fry in fat or oil heated to 350°F., or sauté in butter, for 2 or 3 minutes, or until golden brown.

MAKES 6 CRAB CAKES.

CRÊPES WITH CRAB SAUCE

1 pound fresh backfin crab meat
6 large or 12 small crêpes (see page 21)
3 tablespoons butter or margarine
3 tablespoons flour
1 tablespoon snipped fresh chives
1 tablespoon finely diced green pepper
½ teaspoon salt
⅜ teaspoon freshly ground black pepper
1 cup light cream or half-and-half
1 tablespoon finely chopped onion
¼ teaspoon dry mustard
¼ cup freshly grated Swiss cheese
¼ cup freshly grated Parmesan cheese
¼ cup heavy cream, whipped

Prepare crêpes, stack, and set aside. Remove cartilage from crab meat. In a saucepan, melt butter or margarine, stir in flour, chives, green pepper, salt, and ⅛ teaspoon of the pepper, and blend until smooth. Slowly add light cream or half-and-half. Cook over moderate heat, stirring constantly, until mixture comes to a boil and thickens, about 10 minutes. Remove from heat and add onion, mustard, remaining ¼ teaspoon pepper, and crab meat. Place about ¼ cup crab mixture on each crêpe and fold over. Place crêpes, seam side down, in a greased shallow pan.

In a small bowl, combine Swiss cheese, Parmesan cheese, and whipped cream and mix until well blended. Top crêpes with cheese mixture. Bake in a preheated 375°F. oven for 10 minutes, or until top is browned. Serve at once.

MAKES 6 SERVINGS.

NOTE: *Crêpes, sauce, and topping may be prepared ahead of time, and the recipe may be finished at the time of serving.*

CRAB MEAT ADVENTURE

1 pound fresh lump crab meat
5 tablespoons butter or margarine
1 cup sliced fresh mushrooms
1 cup finely chopped celery
¾ cup sliced water chestnuts
3 large ripe avocados
lemon juice
1 cup cream
1 tablespoon Dijon mustard
1 teaspoon Worcestershire sauce
½ teaspoon sugar
3 drops liquid hot pepper sauce
1 cup mayonnaise
juice of ½ lime
salt to taste
½ cup slivered blanched almonds, toasted
2 tablespoons chopped fresh parsley
1 tablespoon Cognac
garnish: almonds, lemon

Remove cartilage from crab meat. In a skillet, melt 2 tablespoons of the butter or margarine, add mushrooms and celery, and simmer for about 5 minutes, stirring occasionally. Add crab meat and water chestnuts. Cook, stirring, until ingredients are well mixed. Cook, covered, over low heat for about 5 minutes.

Halve avocados lengthwise. Discard pits and rub cut surfaces with lemon juice. Place avocados in a baking dish with ½ inch of hot water and heat in a preheated 400°F. oven for 10 minutes. In a large saucepan, combine the remaining 3 tablespoons butter or margarine, the cream, mustard, Worcestershire sauce, sugar, liquid hot pepper sauce, and mayonnaise. Heat to almost boiling, stirring constantly. Stir in lime juice and salt. Add crab meat mixture and almonds; mix well. Stir in parsley and Cognac. Remove avocados to serving dish. Fill with the hot crab meat mixture and top with additional toasted almonds. Garnish with lemon slices.

MAKES 6 SERVINGS.

CRISFIELD CRAB FONDUE

1 pound fresh crab meat
½ pound cream cheese
6 ounces Gruyère cheese, grated
(1½ cups)
½ cup milk
¼ teaspoon lemon-and-pepper
seasoning
salt and freshly ground pepper
to taste
¼ cup sherry
french bread, cut into 1- to
1½-inch cubes

Remove cartilage from crab meat. In a fondue pot set over low heat, combine cheeses, milk, seasonings, and sherry. Stir until blended and smooth. Add crab meat and heat, stirring occasionally, for 5 to 10 minutes, or until hot and bubbly.

For serving, spear cubes of bread with fondue fork and swirl in figure-eight motion. If fondue thickens on standing, stir in a little additional milk or sherry.

MAKES ABOUT 4 SERVINGS.

NOTE: *If you do not have a fondue pot, mixture may be made in a double boiler and either served from that or transferred to a chafing dish.*

PÂTÉ OF DUNGENESS CRAB WITH SORREL

two 2-pound Dungeness crabs
1 pound sole or salmon fillets
2 eggs
6 ounces cooked fresh mushrooms, pureed
¾ cup heavy cream
4 ounces fresh sorrel, chopped
1 tablespoon minced fresh chervil
1 tablespoon minced fresh chives
1 tablespoon minced fresh tarragon
2 shallots, finely chopped

Drop the crabs into boiling water without seasoning and boil for 20 minutes. Let crabs cool, then pick the meat from the shells. Grind sole or salmon fillets into a large bowl. Add eggs, mushroom puree, cream, sorrel, and minced herbs. In a blender or food processor, puree the mixture, part at a time, then combine all batches together. Stir in crab meat and shallots, and turn into a well-buttered 8-cup terrine. Cook, covered, in a preheated 300°F. oven for 1 hour. Let cool, then refrigerate for 2 hours. Serve cold.

MAKES 8 SERVINGS AS A FIRST COURSE.

CRAB IMPERIAL

1 pound fresh backfin crab meat
3 tablespoons butter or margarine
1 tablespoon flour
½ cup milk
1 teaspoon instant minced onion
1½ teaspoons Worcestershire sauce
2 slices white bread, crusts removed, cubed
½ cup mayonnaise
1 tablespoon lemon juice
½ teaspoon salt
few dashes of freshly ground pepper
garnish: paprika

Remove cartilage from crab meat. In a medium saucepan, melt 1 tablespoon of the butter or margarine; mix in flour. Slowly add milk, stirring constantly to keep mixture smooth and free from lumps. Cook, stirring, over medium heat until mixture comes to a boil and thickens. Mix in onion, Worcestershire sauce, and bread cubes. Let cool. Fold in mayonnaise, lemon juice, salt, and pepper.

In skillet, heat remaining 2 tablespoons butter or margarine until lightly browned. Add crab meat and toss lightly; combine with sauce mixture. Spoon into individual shells or ramekins, or a greased 1-quart casserole. Sprinkle paprika over top. Bake in a preheated 450°F. oven for 10 to 15 minutes, or until hot and bubbly and lightly browned on top.

MAKES 4 SERVINGS.

CRAB AND LEEK TARTS

1 pound fresh blue crab meat
tart pastry for 8 individual tarts
1 pound leeks
½ cup pitted green olives
2 tablespoons oil
¼ cup unsalted butter
6 shallots, minced
½ pound ripe tomatoes, peeled, seeded, and cut into small cubes
3 eggs, separated
1 cup chicken stock
juice of 1 lemon
¼ pound farmer cheese, crumbled
garnish: sliced leeks

Line eight 1-cup tart pans with pastry, crimp or flute the edges, and prick bottoms with a fork. Press foil into the pastry, fill with ceramic pie pellets or dried beans, and bake in a preheated 400°F. oven for 8 minutes, or until pastry is light brown. Let cool.

Pick over crab meat to remove any bits of cartilage. Wash leeks thoroughly, cut into thin round slices, and wash again; pat dry. Blanch olives to remove some of the salt, drain, and chop. In a large skillet, heat oil and butter and sauté shallots and leeks until translucent. Add tomatoes and sauté until mixture is soft. Stir in olives and crab meat; set aside. In a large bowl, beat egg yolks, chicken stock, lemon juice, and cheese until smooth and thick. Stir in the crab and leek mixture. In a separate bowl, beat egg whites until they hold stiff peaks when beater is withdrawn. Gently fold egg whites into crab mixture. Spoon even amounts into the tart shells. Return tart pans to the 400°F. oven and bake for 10 to 15 minutes, or until tart filling is puffed and golden brown.

MAKES 8 SERVINGS AS A FIRST COURSE.

CRAYFISH WITH CHAMPAGNE

24 crayfish
1 cup champagne
1 cup chicken broth
1 carrot, minced
2 shallots, minced
1 clove garlic, minced
1 bay leaf
2 slices lemon
1 sprig fresh parsley
1 sprig fresh thyme
1 sprig fresh chervil
6 peppercorns
garnish: fresh parsley

In a large saucepan, combine all ingredients except crayfish and bring to a boil; reduce heat and simmer, covered, for 30 minutes. Add crayfish and simmer for 12 minutes, or until crayfish are red. Let cool in broth, then chill in refrigerator. Serve cold, garnished with chopped parsley. Accompany with glasses of chilled champagne.

MAKES 2 SERVINGS.

LOBSTER SALAD WITH POPPY SEED DRESSING

1 pound cooked lobster meat
(fresh or frozen)
2 quarts small pieces romaine lettuce
one 11-ounce can mandarin orange
sections, drained
¾ cup thinly sliced celery
½ cup slivered almonds
Poppy Seed Dressing
(recipe follows)

Thaw lobster meat if frozen. Cut lobster meat into ½-inch pieces. Combine lobster, romaine, mandarin orange sections, celery, and almonds; mix well. Make Poppy Seed Dressing, pour over salad, and toss carefully.

MAKES 6 SERVINGS.

Poppy Seed Dressing

¾ cup oil
¼ cup white vinegar
¼ cup honey
¾ teaspoon dry mustard
¾ teaspoon salt
2¼ teaspoons poppy seeds

In a blender, combine oil, vinegar, honey, mustard, and salt; mix well. Add poppy seeds and blend again.

MAKES ABOUT 1 CUP.

LOBSTER-ASPARAGUS SOUP

¾ pound cooked lobster meat
(fresh or frozen)
¼ cup butter or margarine
¼ cup flour
1 tablespoon salt
dash of grated nutmeg
dash of freshly ground pepper
6 cups milk
2 pounds fresh asparagus, or two
10-ounce packages frozen
asparagus spears, cooked,
drained, and diced
3 cups shredded sharp Cheddar
cheese
garnish: paprika

Thaw lobster meat if frozen. Cut lobster meat into ½-inch pieces. In a 4-quart soup pot, melt butter; blend in flour, salt, nutmeg, and pepper. Add milk gradually and cook, stirring constantly, until thickened and smooth. Add lobster, asparagus, and cheese; continue to cook over low heat, stirring occasionally, just until cheese melts and lobster is heated thoroughly. Garnish with paprika. Serve with bread sticks. Serve hot.

MAKES 6 SERVINGS.

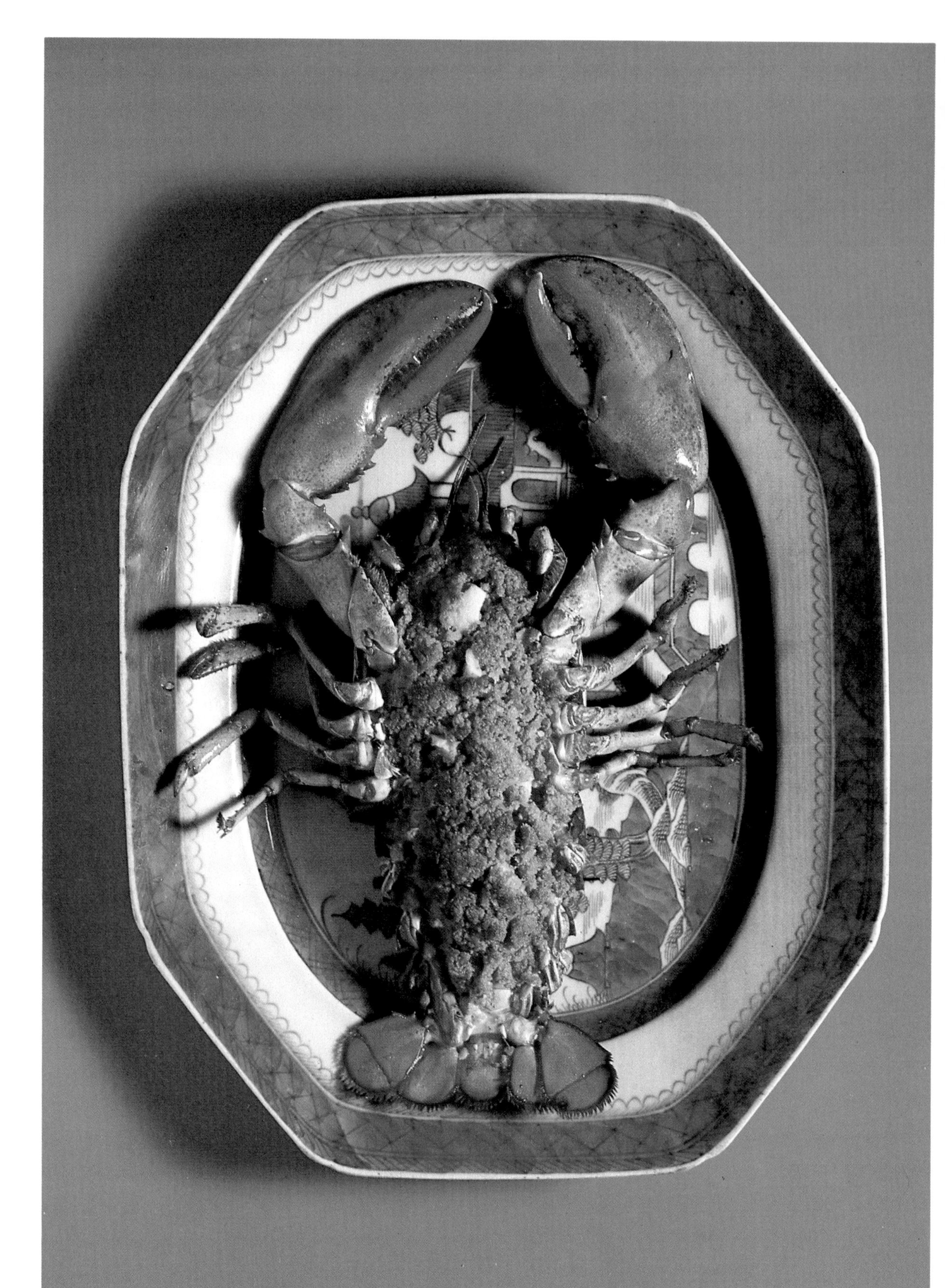

BAKED STUFFED LOBSTER

4 live 1- to 1¼-pound lobsters
3 cups finely ground Ritz crackers
3 cups finely ground white
bread crumbs
4 tablespoons freshly grated cheese
2 large cloves garlic, pressed
2 tablespoons Worcestershire sauce
6 drops Tabasco
2 tablespoons sherry or lemon juice
½ cup clam broth
1 cup clarified butter
10 to 12 ounces small scallops
10 to 12 ounces lobster meat chunks

In a large bowl, mix crackers, bread crumbs, cheese, and garlic. Add Worcestershire sauce, Tabasco, sherry or lemon juice, clam broth, and clarified butter; mix thoroughly. Crumb stuffing should be very moist, but light.

Cut live lobsters from head to tail; remove and discard gills and intestinal vein. Remove tomalley, chop, and add to crumb stuffing. Stuff cavity with scallops and chunked lobster meat. Pack lightly with crumb stuffing, mounding it over the body section. Arrange lobsters on a baking sheet, placing a large potato or weight on the tail. Add water to cover the bottom of the baking sheet. Bake in a preheated 425°F. oven for 20 minutes.

MAKES 4 SERVINGS.

NOTE: *Depending on the size of the lobsters, there may be some stuffing left over (about 1 cup). Mix this with chopped bacon, chopped red pepper, and chopped onion and use to stuff clams. (This makes a "mock" Clams Casino.)*

SHELLFISH IN PATTY SHELLS

1 cup cooked shelled fresh shrimps
1 cup cooked lobster meat
¼ pound bay scallops
¼ cup butter or margarine
¼ cup flour
1 small ripe tomato, peeled and chopped
½ cup champagne
1½ cups heavy cream
salt and freshly ground pepper
to taste
6 baked patty shells
garnish: seedless green grapes

In a saucepan, melt butter and stir in flour. Stir in tomato and champagne; then gradually stir in cream. Cook, stirring, over low heat until sauce thickens and bubbles. Season with salt and pepper. Stir in shrimps, lobster meat, and scallops. Reheat until bubbly. Spoon mixture into patty shells. Serve garnished with seedless green grapes.

MAKES 6 SERVINGS AS A FIRST COURSE.

HANNAH MARINER'S PIE

18 ounces mixed cooked shellfish meat (scallops, shrimps, lobster, and crab), broth reserved
1 to 1½ cups sliced fresh mushrooms
2 tablespoons chopped fresh chives
¼ cup mayonnaise
¾ cup sour cream
2 cups light cream
½ teaspoon salt
¼ teaspoon freshly ground white pepper
1 tablespoon Worcestershire sauce
½ teaspoon crumbled dried thyme
5 tablespoons butter
5 tablespoons flour
1 teaspoon paprika
3 ounces brandy
1½ ounces sherry
approximately ½ cup reserved shellfish broth
garnish: parsley sprig

In the top part of a double boiler set over hot water, combine mushrooms, chives, mayonnaise, sour cream, light cream, salt, pepper, Worcestershire sauce, and thyme. Warm, but do not boil. In a small saucepan, melt butter and sprinkle with flour and paprika. Cook roux over low heat for 2 minutes, blending thoroughly. Bring the water in the bottom of the double boiler to steaming in order to blend sauce ingredients. When the mixture is quite hot (160° to 180°F.), add the roux all at once, otherwise the sour cream will separate. Mix well. Add the cooked shellfish, the brandy, and the sherry. Thin to a velvety consistency with as much of the shellfish broth as needed. Spoon into six individual casserole dishes.

MAKES 6 SERVINGS.

BOURRIDE

1 live lobster
2 meaty crabs
fish heads and scraps for stock
1 sea bass, dressed and boned
1 pound shrimps, shelled and deveined
1 pound sea scallops, halved
¼ cup olive oil
1 large carrot, minced
1 large globe onion, sliced
2 large leeks, sliced
2 large cloves garlic, minced
4 quarts fish stock
3 large ripe tomatoes, peeled and chopped
¾ cup Amontillado sherry
1 large bay leaf
1 bouquet garni
2 pieces bitter-orange rind, minced
¼ teaspoon ground saffron
1½ pounds fresh green beans, cut
salt to taste

Drop live lobster into boiling salted water and cook until it turns pink; reserve cooking liquid. Shell crab and lobster bodies, leaving legs and claws whole; refrigerate until ready to use. Add fish heads and scraps to reserved lobster cooking liquid, adding more water if necessary to make 6 quarts. Bring to a boil, reduce heat, and simmer for 2 hours, or until stock is reduced by one-fourth (leaving 4½ quarts). Strain through double thicknesses of cheesecloth; reserve.

Pour oil into a soup pot or Dutch oven large enough to hold all the fish and stock later. Over low heat, cook carrot, onion, leeks, and garlic only until just tender. Add last nine ingredients and simmer for about 15 minutes to allow flavors to marry. Bring to a boil, add all the seafoods except the lobster, and cook for about 8 minutes, or until shrimps are pink and scallops tender. Do not overcook. Add lobster pieces and cook only to heat through. Remove bay leaf and bouquet garni. Serve with hot garlic bread and glasses of chilled Amontillado sherry.

MAKES 8 TO 10 SERVINGS.

JEREZ-XERES-
SHERRY

YOSENABE

one 1- to 1½-pound lobster, cut into bite-size pieces
6 to 8 large prawns, shelled and deveined
6 to 8 sea scallops, quartered, or 12 to 16 bay scallops, halved
12 to 16 cherrystone clams, shucked
2 to 4 young carrots, cut into thin diagonal pieces
8 to 10 scallions, cut into thin diagonal pieces
½ pound *harusame* (cellophane noodles), or 1 can *shiratake* (yam-flour noodles)
6 to 8 cups rich chicken stock or delicate fish stock, preheated

Blanch shellfish in salted boiling water for no more than 10 to 12 seconds; drain and quickly cool under cold running water. Blanch carrots in salted boiling water for 1 minute; drain and quickly cool under running water.

Soak *harusame* in cold water until soft, about 30 minutes; boil for about 12 minutes, drain, and place in an attractive bowl. Or use *shiratake* as they come from the can. Both varieties of noodles are very long and can be cut to more manageable lengths.

Make Yosenabe Dipping Sauce (recipe follows). Arrange shellfish and vegetables in attractive designs on one or two large plates or a lacquered Japanese tray. Place individual bowls, chopsticks, and sauce bowls at each place setting. Use an appropriate self-contained electric, alcohol, or Sterno burner. Pour chicken stock into a large casserole, set on the burner, and keep at a simmer throughout the meal. The diners make their food choices and, using chopsticks, cook their own food for 3 to 5 minutes; the cooked food is then dipped into individual sauce bowls, each containing ½ cup dipping sauce.

Noodles can be heated all at once, to be lifted into diners' bowls to be eaten along with the shellfish and vegetables. Finally, the enriched broth is ladled into the bowls for drinking at the end of the meal in traditional fashion.

MAKES 6 SERVINGS.

Yosenabe Dipping Sauce

Combine 1 cup soy sauce; 1 cup fresh lemon juice; ½ cup daikon, or other strong radish, grated; 4 or 5 scallions, thinly sliced; and 2 or 3 drops Tabasco. Heat ½ cup fino sherry, let cool, and add to mixture. Serve sauce in small individual bowls.

MAKES ABOUT 3 CUPS.

INDEX

Not
Renewable